Basically ...

GEMMA COLLINS

Basically...

MY LIFE AS A
REAL ESSEX GIRL

EBURY
PRESS

1 3 5 7 9 10 8 6 4 2

This edition published 2013
First published in 2013 by Ebury Press, an imprint of Ebury Publishing
A Random House Group company

The Random House Group Limited Reg. No. 954009

Addresses for companies within the Random House Group can be found at
www.randomhouse.co.uk

A CIP catalogue record for this book is available from the British Library

The Random House Group Limited supports the Forest Stewardship
Council® (FSC®), the leading international forest-certification organisation.
Our books carrying the FSC label are printed on FSC®-certified paper. FSC
is the only forest-certification scheme supported by the leading environmental
organisations, including Greenpeace. Our paper procurement policy can be found
at www.randomhouse.co.uk/environment

Designed and set by seagulls.net

Printed and bound by CPI Group (UK) Ltd, Croydon, CR0 4YY

ISBN 9780091955632

To buy books by your favourite authors and register for offers visit
www.randomhouse.co.uk

To Mum and Dad. I am everything I am because you love me. And to Russell and Dawn who I love and thank you for giving me the two best things in my life, Kane and Hayden. I never knew the power of love until these two came along.

ABOUT THE AUTHOR

Gemma Collins hails from Romford, Essex and is a star of the ITV2 reality show *The Only Way Is Essex*. Having attended the Sylvia Young Theatre School as a child, Gemma was always destined to become a star. At a very early age she was noticed by industry moguls and went on to secure starring roles in theatre productions such as *The Sound of Music*.

Gemma makes regular appearances on TV shows like *This Morning* and *8 Out of 10 Cats* as well as in national magazines and newspapers. More recently, she has launched her own global clothing line, The Gemma Collins Collection which you can find at www.gemmacollinsofficial.com. She is managed by Can Management. Gemma is a girl who is never afraid to speak her mind. She is straight talking, outspoken and confident. This is her first book.

CONTENTS

This book contains glamour, hot men, flash cars, Jacuzzi sex, heartache, nightclubs, a romp in a field and false eyelashes. Some of the names you read might be fake, but the people and situations are all real.

CHAPTER ONE

MADE IN DAGENHAM

Basically, it started at a bus stop in Dagenham. It was a proper East End love story. Boy meets girl. Girl isn't that interested. Boy persists. Girl gives in. I was the result.

If you don't know Dagenham, let me give you a flavour of the place. It's a large suburb in east London about halfway between the Essex countryside and the centre of the capital. It's fair to say that it's not the nicest place in the world: it's grimy, it's built-up and it has more than its fair share of kebab shops and bargain-booze outlets. But the people there are the salt of the earth. It's where the people from the poor parts of the East End head to when they've made a few quid; a halfway house between London's council estates and the gated mansions and exclusive apartment complexes of Essex.

Dagenham's claim to fame is the Ford assembly plant, a sprawling factory that, in its heyday, churned out cars such as the Cortina and the Fiesta. The movie *Made in Dagenham* is about a strike that happened at the plant, when the women workers who stitched together the upholstery for the cars brought the assembly line to a halt in a battle with management over equal pay. The women worked just as hard as the men but got only got a fraction of the pay, and eventually they decided that enough was enough. Dagenham people don't shy away from speaking their minds and sticking up for themselves and they still have that fighting spirit today – as well as an affinity for Ford cars, which must be in their blood.

Several years after the women of Dagenham made themselves famous for their refusal to be paid less than their men, another working girl was standing at a bus stop having a bit of man trouble of her own. She was my mum, Joan. At the time she was a hair-dresser. She was on her way home from a day in the salon and love would have been the last thing on her mind. She was probably looking forward to dinner and an early night.

Joan had had a tough life.

She was born in Lambeth Hospital and lived in a place called Barnes, which was, and still is, a very posh, leafy village on the River Thames in west London. She didn't have a chance to enjoy the benefits of her place of birth, however, because she was abandoned by her own mother after she was born. She was named by the hospital and at two weeks old was sent to live with a foster family in Dagenham, which is at the opposite end of the District Line on the London Underground but may as well be at the opposite end of the earth. From what I know, Mum's mum – my gran – was young and unmarried when she got pregnant and in those days that was seen as shameful. Young single mums were sent away to homes to have their babies and more often than not the babies were fostered out or taken on by older members of the family. Mum never knew her mother. I often wonder how that would have felt and how it's affected her. I'm incredibly close to my mother: we are best friends. Together with my dad, she's been there to support me through every stage of my life, good and bad. I couldn't imagine not having that presence in my life so, knowing that, I think it must have been tough on my mum to know that she was unwanted.

Mum never tried to trace her own mother. She is not bitter about it. I suppose she figured that there's nothing to be gained from knowing the woman who abandoned her. But she did know her dad. He kept in contact with her after she was fostered out and he used to visit her now and again until he left the UK. He now lives in Australia.

So it was a hard start for a young girl and things didn't get any easier. When she was still young her foster-mother died, and a terrible period in her life began, where her future was uncertain. No one knew what to do with her. Mum says one of her first memories was of sitting on a chair when she was about five or six with her foster-father's adult children. She remembers them looking at her and saying 'What are we going to do with Joan, should we put her in a home?' Although Mum has a lovely life now, that situation must have been awful for her. She must have been terrified hearing those words and having that uncertainty hanging over her. Eventually her foster-mother's daughter, Sylvie, took her on. Sylvie was married to a lovely guy called Les and they had three children already: Julie, David and Deborah. They looked after her, included her and loved and cared for her. They all share a special bond, and I will always love my Dagenham family for looking after my mum.

That was the girl at the bus stop. The boy was my dad; Alan Collins, a young man from Dagenham with a spring in his step and a head full of dreams. He wanted a better life and a nice Ford. Both Mum and Dad came from families where money was in short supply. My paternal grandparents were originally from Wales and

Dad told me once that when he was growing up his family were so poor they used to lick the grease off the newspaper their chips were wrapped in to keep warm. I'm sure he was being over the top though! He lived in a council house in Dagenham and worked in a shipping firm. There are huge docks in the east of London and at that time a lot of families from across the country moved to the area to find work, Dad's included.

The day he saw my mum at the bus stop his heart skipped a beat – well, at least that's what I like to think. He was looking out of a window that overlooked the road Mum was standing on, clapped eyes on her (she was and still is a good-looking woman) and, being the ever-hopeful person he was, he ran outside, approached her and asked her if she wanted a lift home. She said no. She might not have had much money but she had standards and she wasn't going to go out with any old riff-raff off the street. Dad wasn't put off by this early rejection; over the following days he kept his eye out for the lady at the stop and whenever she turned up he would find an excuse to chat to her. Nowadays if someone behaved like that you would get a restraining order! Thankfully the harassment laws were more lenient back then.

Slowly, Dad's charm and gyver (that's an Essex word that means 'front') won her round and when he eventually asked if she wanted to go on a date she agreed. Their first night out was spent at a local pub and Dad soon found out that Mum had expensive tastes. When he asked her what she wanted to drink she ordered up a Dagenham cocktail; a large brandy and Babycham, the most expensive drink the pub served at the time. Dad had neglected to tell her that he was skint – that one round wiped him out. He could just about afford a half a lager for himself and nursed it all night, worried that Mum might ask for another drink and that he'd have to confess that he had no money left.

Despite the money problems Joan and Alan got on famously and soon became a couple. The rest is history. They married, in 1978 they had a son, Russell, and on January 31 1981 Joan Collins gave birth to me. I was born in Old Church Hospital, Romford and I was out to shock from day one.

The very first words I ever heard were 'Oh My God', which is quite fitting when you consider what's happened in my later life. Apparently that's what the midwife exclaimed when she first saw me. Mum thought she had given birth to a baby with two heads.

I can picture the scene now, Mum lying there half delirious and bathed in sweat and the midwife gasping in shock.

'What's wrong with my baby?' Mum would have asked, panicked.

Thankfully there was no problem. The midwife was just shocked because I was such a long baby. I was massive: I only weighed 7lbs 8oz but I was the longest baby she had ever seen. The average baby is between 19 and 21 inches long but I was 25 inches. I'm not sure why I was so tall; neither of my parents are. My mum is 5ft 6ins and Dad is just slightly taller.

Mum was over the moon that she had had a little girl. She said I was the most perfect baby she could have wished for. I slept well, I ate well, I was well-behaved and I didn't cry very much. Mum would often comment to Dad that I was too good to be true. When I was a newborn she would look at me in my cot and tell him how lucky they both were. Mum made a vow to herself that she would always be there for both me and my brother and that she would always protect us and put us first. Having missed out on the love of a birth mother, she was determined that we would always feel wanted. She knew more than anyone what abandonment felt like.

Joan had a feeling that all the peace and quiet wouldn't last for ever. She was right – when I got to three everything changed and I went from being a quiet, contented baby to a whining, whingeing monster. As Mum remembers it, I cried all the time. Someone only had to say my name and I would bawl. It got to the point where one day Mum started crying too. She was so frustrated. She didn't know what had happened to me. There was nothing wrong with me medically, I was just ridiculously oversensitive. I had become a diva!

Apparently the crying phase lasted for several years. It was a tough time for my parents. Mum gave up full-time work after Russell was born but still worked part time doing hair when Russell and I were young. Dad worked all the hours he could and money was tight. He still managed to take us on holidays but they were nearly always to places nearby in the UK, such as Clacton-on-Sea. I did have a taste of early glamour once though. When I was a baby we went to the south of France in a VW Camper, Jamie Oliver-style. The first family car we had, however, was a Ford Orion. It was the first of many Fords I can remember our family having; you can take the man out of Dagenham, but you can't take Dagenham out of the man!

Dad was always very careful with money. He still is. He has always lived within his means and apart from the necessities like the mortgage, he has never relied on credit or borrowed beyond his means. Even now he tells me never to be flash.

'It gets you nowhere, Gem,' he says. 'As long as you work and you can pay the bills you don't have to prove yourself to anyone. Money can be a poison, don't get attracted to it.'

His advice has stuck. Don't get me wrong, I've had money problems over the years (more of that later) and I love my clothes and I love a bit of glam, but sometimes I rock up in a crappy old pair of leggings with holes in them and I'm not bothered what people think. As long as I can pay the bills and I own what I have, as far as I'm concerned, I haven't got to prove anything to anyone.

Dad will make a pair of shoes last for three years and he can tell you how much each pair he owns cost. He is even able to tell you how long he has owned them, divide that by what they cost and calculate which have been the best value for money!

There was never much spare money around when I was really little. Dad took on extra jobs on top of his regular one to make ends meet. At one time he worked a full-time day job and also a part-time job in a bar, just so he could feed and clothe Russell and me. He rarely treats himself and he looks after everything he owns; always has. He only has about five polo shirts in his wardrobe but because he's financially comfortable now, he's gone from Marks and Spencer to Ralph Lauren! He loves those shirts and he irons them himself. Even though ironing is generally Mum's job.

All Mum and Dad have ever wanted is a good life for their children and so, although they could barely afford it, before Russell and I were born they moved out of Dagenham and headed east into the Essex borders. I can't remember the first house we lived in because I was just a baby and we weren't there for long. It was in the suburbs, a place called Collier Row. When I was a few years old they moved again, to a place nearby called Rise Park, also in Essex. They still live in the same house now.

Rise Park is a nice area; not top dollar but not run-down. Decent, strait-laced, working people lived there. There were no crooks and villains. The community was made up of people doing well for themselves and getting on in life. When we moved in as a young family the neighbours didn't have enough money for luxury Mercedes or BMWs; instead there were Fords everywhere. It was quiet – nothing flash; no big mansions with swimming pools, just normal suburban family homes. There was a park there and a lovely little school, which I started going to when I was old enough. It was a very safe and nice place to live.

Our three-bedroom house was basic. We didn't have central heating or the luxury of wall-to-wall carpets. The flooring in the lounge consisted of squares of carpet and wooden boards. It used to get cold in the winters and the lounge would be heated with an old-fashioned gas fire. One of my first memories is of sitting on the rug in front of the fire and toasting bread. I would stick a slice of Mother's Pride on a fork and hold it up to the heat. We couldn't afford a toaster.

Pride of place in the lounge was the family three-piece suite. It was black PVC and Dad had bought it second-hand – he gave a lady £5 for it when she was about to chuck it out. It had a split in it, which Mum patched up, and she used to polish it so you could see your face in it.

My parents decorated my bedroom for me and it was very girlie, which I loved although I was never much into dolls and Barbies. I had a few though, and I remember having a toy pram that I would push around, but one Christmas I was bought a massive Sindy doll's house and never played with it. Mum got rid of it in January. She wasn't one for clutter.

The kitchen was small with hardly any worktops and bright orange Formica units. Mum jokes today that she can prepare a meal in any tightly confined space.

'Just give me the top of a fridge or a tray and I can work on it,' she says. It's a skill she learned in that old, cramped kitchen.

Mum was a good cook and always made sure there was a dinner on the table for the whole family. We ate home-cooked food and Mum made sure what we had went as far as it could. We would have a chicken and Mum would make it last for three days: we'd have a roast dinner, then the next day Mum would make what was left into chicken sandwiches, and finally she'd pick the remains off the bird and make a chicken soup for the following day.

Although we were hard up, I don't remember ever going without. My parents always made sure we had what we needed. We didn't always get what we wanted, but we were loved and looked after. We would also have family treats, although nothing flashy or expensive.

Partly this was because there wasn't much choice in the way of shopping in Rise Park. There were no flash designer boutiques or luxury spas such as you see in *TOWIE*. The highlight of my shopping expeditions in those days was a Saturday trip to Woolworths with Mum. It was a regular event and one I loved. I'd flick through the rails filled with Woolies' own-brand childrens' wear, Ladybird, and pick out outfits I thought looked good. I can still remember some of the clothes. One day I saw a pair of baby-blue and pink fluffy slippers on the shelves and from the moment I set my four-year-old eyes on them I just had to have them. I've had plenty of shoes since, but those slippers are branded into my memory. They were Disney Princess Cinderella slippers and were finished off with a puff of fluff. I pestered Mum for weeks to let me have those slippers and the day she agreed, I felt like I had won the lottery. They probably only cost about £1 but they were a bit of glamour in my life and I reckon they were what gave me my love of shoes in later life.

I had a thing about fake fur and fluff. I developed a strange habit and hankering for it. When I was taken out shopping I would make a beeline for any fluffy dressing gowns, suck my thumb and twiddle the fluff around on my nose! Apparently I did that every time we went shopping.

I sucked my thumb for many years. Mum was forever fretting that I would end up with crooked teeth because of it. My thumbnail would get worn down and my thumb became all wrinkled where I'd sucked it so much. I was in my late teens when I eventually kicked the habit but obviously by then I wouldn't suck it in public.

When we weren't shopping in Woolies at the weekend we would often go out for family dinners, on a Friday or Saturday night. We'd get dressed up – me in my fluffy slippers, Dad in his polo shirt – and we'd head to Rise Park's finest restaurant: the Wimpy. We couldn't afford expensive meals in some of the more fashionable restaurants in neighbouring towns such as Chigwell and Buckhurst Hill, but I didn't care as long as I could spend time with my family and scoff Wimpy's famous Brown Derby pudding, which was a doughnut topped with ice cream.

Basically, when I reflect on it now, I know that even though there wasn't much money around, my childhood was filled with love and I only have very happy memories of my first years in Essex.

CHAPTER TWO

EARLY DAYS

he first school I went to was Rise Park Infants School just down the road from where I lived. By all accounts there were no nerves on my first day – I was up early, excited and raring to go. I had all my pens and pencils organised and Mum had spent the night before cleaning and pressing my uniform to make sure it was crisp, clean and tidy. She's always been a big believer in making an impression and although all the children at the school wore the same grey and green uniform, she wanted me to stand out. She was a perfectionist and has always encouraged me to look my best. I was always immaculate as a child; from my clean, brushed hair to my shoes, which Mum would polish religiously every night when I got home from school.

I would be sent in each day wearing a clean, pressed uniform, shiny shoes and bright white socks. Mum didn't have much in the way of possessions when she was growing up so she always looked after what she had, and she wanted Russell and me to look good and have the very best she could afford.

At Rise Park school I met my first best friend, Vicky Rance. We have remained close since. When she was at infant school she was ever so slight; there was nothing of her. We hit it off straight away and became mates inside and outside of school. Our parents would ferry us between each others' houses at the weekend so we could hang out together. Vicky lived in a big house in a neighbourhood called Gidea Park, but when she was young her parents got divorced and she had to leave the large house and move to a smaller one. She was a lovely girl and even during that tough family time she just got on with it and enjoyed life.

At home, I had a typical brother and sister relationship with Russell. He was a few years older than me, so he had already started school and made friends. Most weekends he was off doing boy stuff with them and I would either meet Vicky or be left with my mum. I wouldn't say I was the best of friends with Russell when I was young; we used to argue, but then I suppose all siblings do. Russell liked to play practical jokes and he liked to wind me up. Older brothers seem to have a talent for finding weaknesses in their sisters to exploit and Russell discovered mine early on: the dark. I always preferred to go to sleep with a nightlight on, or a light left on in the hallway. Russell knew this and so, on several occasions, decided to capitalise on it. Just before my bedtime he would sneak quietly into my room and hide under my bed. I would get tucked in and begin to drift off to sleep. Russell, still as a statue underneath me, would give me ten minutes to settle in and listen out for when my breathing became deeper, an indication that I was going to sleep. And as I did he would begin making low howling noises. I'd wake, startled, from my half-sleep, confused and terrified. It always took me a few minutes to realise what was going on and for it to register that it was my brother playing tricks and in those bewildering minutes my heart would race. I would be convinced there was a werewolf in the room with me. I laugh about it now, but it's funny how things that happen to you when you are young can affect you in later life. Even now I am petrified of the dark and I was thirty years old when I finally plucked up the courage to sleep with the light off, thanks to Russell.

We were always protected from what was going on around us. It was as though Mum and Dad had placed a protective bubble around us. Mum says today that if she was allowed her way she would have home-schooled me. When I was little she wanted to keep me close and keep me safe, and so we went through our early childhood unaware of the financial hardships our parents were enduring. Dad was struggling to make ends meet, even with two jobs. He commuted from where we lived to the firm he worked at and would be exhausted most of the time. Mum was finding it harder and harder to keep me looking immaculate and eventually the breaking point came – over a pair of shoes. I needed them but Dad couldn't afford them. Mum told him something had to give.

'You work all the hours under the sun and you can't afford to put a new pair of shoes on Gemma's feet,' I remember her saying. 'What's going on?'

Whenever anyone first meets my mum they assume that she's quiet and reserved, but she is actually the backbone of the family and tells it like it is. She was tired of watching her husband work himself to exhaustion for someone else's benefit.

'You are more than capable, Alan,' she told him. 'You are determined and you are a hard worker and it's about time you put that to good use and set up business on your own.'

They had no money themselves to start a business so they went to my paternal grandfather and asked him for a loan. He was also hard up but he had faith in his son and he loaned Dad £4000 to rent some warehouse space in the Isle of Dogs, which was an industrial area of east London. That's where Dad started up his own shipping company, Transforwarding Ltd. It was a big step for him and he made it his mission to pay back every penny he had been lent.

Mum made a vow to Dad that while he worked hard on establishing and developing his business, she would go without luxuries for as long as it took. She tells me that she went without new shoes for two years and I recall vividly that most nights I would see her polishing her only pair. She loved those shoes. She made sure they lasted: we used to have a polish cupboard filled with every colour of polish you could imagine. Every penny Dad earned was put towards paying off the loan or was ploughed back into the business as an investment.

I didn't understand back then what he did and how the business worked, and I still don't if I'm honest. Soon, though, it started to make money. My dad turned a profit and used it to grow the business. From the outside, however, no one would have known because we stayed in the same modest house and none of the money went on home improvements. Mum continued cooking in her cramped kitchen and the old second-hand three-piece suite continued to take pride of place on the floorboards in the lounge. Dad was ultra-careful; he knew what it was like to have nothing and he didn't want to be in that position again. That's why he has always been against flash spending. When it comes to money he's not your average Essex boy is Dad. But that doesn't mean he isn't prone to gestures of great generosity.

We used to go to Potters holiday camp in Great Yarmouth most years and one year my parents said that Vicky could come along too. They knew she was having a difficult time at home and they thought it would be good for her to come away and have a carefree week in Norfolk with us. Unbeknown to me at the time, when we got there Dad slipped her a £20 note so she could buy ice cream and souvenirs, but he told her not to tell me in case I wanted some money too. It wasn't that he was trying to exclude me. He just knew that I was looked after all year round and he didn't want me to start expecting money without earning it.

Dad worked six days a week, sometimes seven if he was especially busy. He couldn't pick and choose when he went to work; it was his own business and the more he put in, the more he got out. I remember him taking himself off to work even when he was very ill. He didn't have the luxury of sick pay. If he didn't go in, he didn't earn. One year he caught a terrible cold that wouldn't shift and developed into pneumonia. I had never seen him so ill and for a time he went to work half dead; even then he still worked hard – Mum told me he would lie on the office floor taking calls.

After a while, when the business could afford it, Dad took on some staff. There were two men who worked in the warehouse, who were like a double act. I think their names were Bob and Bill. He also had a guard dog called Cookie. It was a great big shaggy Alsatian. It looked fearsome but I loved it.

Watching Dad get up and go off to work every Saturday gave me the flavour. I wanted to be his sidekick and I figured that he was spending so much time at his business, it must have been a fun place to be at the weekends. So I started begging him to let me go and work with him.

At first he wasn't sure. He reasoned that an industrial unit on the Isle of Dogs wasn't the best place for a young girl to be spending her weekends. But I have always been persistent and I kept chipping away at him until eventually he relented.

'Oh go on then,' he sighed, 'as long as you promise to stay out of trouble.' I nodded in agreement.

Having bagged myself a Saturday job at the age of seven, the first problem I had was what did I wear? I wanted to make sure that I impressed. I needed to power-dress. For weeks on our shopping trips to Woolworths, I had been pestering Mum to buy me a neon pink off-the-shoulder top and a pair of cut-off shorts that I reckoned would go well with my Princess slippers. Mum said they looked cheap but I made enough of a fuss that finally she gave in. So that was my work outfit. I customised the top with badges, which were fashionable at the time, and early in the morning I jumped in the family car and headed off to work with Dad. It all felt very grown-up and I couldn't have been happier.

Even as a young girl I had all the confidence in the world and I soon made friends with Bob and Bill, who would give me their cheese sandwiches and cups of tea from their flasks. If I am honest, my presence in the business didn't add a great deal to the productivity of the place. Dad would be working in his office and I would just amuse myself in the warehouse. I may have shuffled some papers around from time to time to look busy, but I never did any actual work.

Soon after I started my Saturday job the business had expanded to the point that the pressure on Dad was becoming immense. He needed to take on more people, and so Peter and Violet arrived, to work in the office.

Violet was massive; as big as three chairs, and her personality was larger than life as well. She also had a biscuit habit! I found this out one day when I was sneaking through her desk and discovered a stash of goodies piled up in one of the drawers. There were packets and packets of them. I couldn't help myself and regularly nicked a couple to munch on. It was my secret for several weeks until Dad caught me with one and asked where I'd got it from. I couldn't lie and told him the truth. I knew it was wrong but I tried to justify it by telling him that Violet had plenty and wouldn't notice if a few went missing. But Dad has always been honest and explained to me that what I was doing was wrong.

The next weekend came and Violet was in the office. I loved mischief and on this day I decided to play a trick on her; I assumed she would go along with it and would enjoy the giggle, because she was a laugh and I really liked her.

I waited for my chance and got it when Violet went off to use the loo. My plan was to creep up on her in there and make her jump. When I heard the door lock I crept up behind it and hid. As Violet opened it I jumped out on her and roared as loud as I could. She staggered backwards, shrieked and clutched her chest. She went pale. As I mentioned before, she was a big woman and I think the shock of me in my neon-pink top jumping out on her may have put a strain on her heart. For an awful moment it looked like she was going to collapse. After a few seconds though she composed herself and, far from laughing at my trick, she stared at me with anger. I could tell I was in trouble.

'I... I... I... was only joking,' I stuttered.

Violet shook her head. The colour was coming back into her face and her cheeks were flushed.

'That is not funny Gemma,' she scolded.

Dad had heard her screams and came running to see what the commotion was about. When Violet told him about my trick he looked at me sternly and gave me a good telling-off. He'd only just taken on new staff. He wouldn't have been pleased if his daughter had killed one of them off before her probationary period was up.

'It's not good to play tricks on people, Gemma,' he told me, wagging his finger.

I stood there with my head bowed, taking the telling-off but feeling like I was the victim of a miscarriage of justice. It was supposed to be a laugh. Violet watched as I got my talking-to and when Dad had finished she turned and went back to her work, satisfied that I had been taught a lesson. Dad too turned sternly away and walked back to his office. But as he did he looked round at me, smiled cheekily and gave me a wink. He liked a laugh too and I knew he had thought it was funny, he just couldn't say so in front of Violet.

CHAPTER THREE

A STAR IS BORN

'You're going to be famous one day Gemma, I can feel it.' Mum was convinced. When she got one of her feelings they usually turned out to be right. I didn't realise at the time but she had a gift. Basically, she was psychic. She had heightened intuitiveness and the uncanny ability to read situations before they happened. When I was about five years old she started to tell me that I would find fame and fortune when I got older. And she believed it wholeheartedly.

I started to notice from quite an early age that I shared her psychic sensitivity. I had the gift. I sensed things, was able to feel presences around me and got flashes of intuition. For example, my brother Russell once introduced me to his new girlfriend Dawn and I knew immediately that she was the girl he would marry. I saw their wedding in my head and I told him straight away: 'Russell, she's the one – you're going to marry her and have a family.'

Over the years I've seen psychics and had readings and my grandparents have come through to me several times. Back in Rise Park when I was a little girl I would sit at the top of the stairs and listen to noises. I've always felt that there are spirits around me and that I am tuned in to their energy. Mum and Dad are quite spiritual, and when I was growing up they meditated and talked about the afterlife and things like that, so in our house it just seemed like a natural part of life. I was rarely scared, just curious. It always felt comforting and friendly; I never felt that there was bad energy in the house. Except once. I was eight years old and I was in Mum's bedroom. She was in the bathroom next door and I was sitting on the bed talking to her. As I was chatting to her I got a very strange feeling. All the hairs on the back of my neck stood up. It was that feeling you get when someone 'walks over your grave', as the phrase goes. I was facing the wardrobe and inside I could see shoeboxes, stacked up on the top shelf. Suddenly one of the boxes flew across the room. It didn't fall. It was launched. It whizzed past my head and hit the wall behind me. The shock made me sit bolt upright and I started screaming hysterically. Mum came running out the bathroom to see what the commotion was about but when she asked me what had happened I was in such a state I wasn't making any sense. I was just howling and blubbing. Eventually she had to grab me and talk to me sternly to make me calm down. Even though she was psychic and believed in ghosts, she thought I was being overdramatic. Nothing bad like that ever happened again in the house and I have no idea where that burst of negative energy came from or what it had against Mum's shoes, but my psychic antennae have remained with me all my life and I often rely on my intuitive feelings to guide me. And Mum always has too, which is why, after she convinced herself I was going to be the next Madonna, she enrolled me in dancing lessons.

I was sent to Everett Dance Academy for my introduction to show business, and I loved it there. I had always been outgoing and enjoyed a bit of attention. I would do song and dance routines for my family in the front room and the academy gave me the chance to express myself. I did ballet, street dance; every style. The lessons became a regular weekend fixture. They coincided with the period when Dad's business had started to do well and he had some spare cash coming in. My parents were still very careful and they didn't blow money on flash things, but Mum wanted me to have the kind of childhood she'd never had, even if it meant her going without a new sofa or new kitchen units. She would rather spend the money on her kids than on herself. She had been close to the church community when she was younger and had enjoyed singing and dancing in the church hall, but never had the chance to pursue her ambitions. She is quite reserved but I reckon secretly she would have loved to have been a performer. And so, with a bit of financial freedom and an instinctive voice in her head telling her I was going to be a star, she passed those ambitions on to me.

Soon after starting dance lessons I decided I wanted to act as well, so I joined a stage school called Harlequins and then one called Theatretrain where I stayed for several years. The man who ran it, Kevin, became a family friend. I was engrossed in the world of performing. I would sing all the time and developed a good voice. On a few occasions I would get told off at school for singing in class but I was generally a very good pupil and never got in any serious trouble. Vicky and I stuck together all the time and although I had plenty of friends I knuckled down and I worked hard. I was never good at maths – but Mum would tell me not to worry too much because I would be famous one day. Dad, on the other hand, was the more practical one and although he was fully supportive of my extra-curricular activities, he also encouraged me to stretch myself academically. Mum would tell him, 'Alan, Gemma has dance class in the morning, don't tire her out by making her work too hard.' He used to have patience and sit down and try to work through my maths homework with me. I had trouble with numbers and struggled with telling the time until I was around eight or nine years old. Dad bought me a special time puzzle that he would do with me to help me learn.

My best subject was history. I did a project on Richard III and I loved doing the research and imagining what it would have been like to live in those times. Another time I chose a more contemporary subject. I had to write a piece on a famous person and I chose my heroine, Madonna. I also saw that it was an opportunity to combine the delivery of the project with some theatrics. As I was reading Madonna's biographical details to the class I broke off mid-flow, jumped up from my chair and started singing 'Vogue'.

My confidence grew and grew, thanks to dancing and acting lessons, and it didn't go unnoticed. When the school was looking for a pupil to deliver a speech in front of the mayor at the county hall I was chosen. It was a real honour and I think Mum was more excited than I was. I can't remember what the subject was – I think it was about recycling in Romford – but I was picked up from home in the mayor's black car with a flag showing the crest of Essex on the front. I was taken to the council debating chamber and stood in front of the audience. I wasn't nervous, I was excited. The thrill of having a room full of dignitaries hanging on my every word was something I can still remember, and I even got a write-up in the local newspaper, the *Romford Recorder*.

My weeks were mapped out for me. Monday to Friday were school days and on Saturday I went to dance and theatre lessons. Mum finished off the rota by booking me pony-riding lessons on a Sunday. It was a seven-day-a-week operation. I was always busy. Mum must have been worried that I would get bored so life was a whirl of activity. On Saturday evenings we would either go out for a meal as a family or stay in, get a takeaway and watch TV together. As the business started to do well our trips to the Wimpy were replaced with trips to local Chinese or Indian restaurants.

When I got a little older I started to go with Mum on her trips to London. It became a regular fixture and it's where my love affair with the city started.

Mum went into town whenever she could and her passion was shopping. She was never one of the typical Essex housewives later made famous by *TOWIE* who would spend fortunes, but she loved window-shopping and browsing. She could spend a whole day on Oxford Street and return home with the same amount of money in her purse as when she'd left in the morning. She just loved the buzz of the city and the glamour of the shops.

Her real luxury was spending money on us children and, around the time I started junior school, I started to become aware of an improvement in my wardrobe. Slowly the Ladybird clothes that I had badgered Mum for in the past were getting replaced by more expensive outfits. It wasn't that Mum had bundles of money and she certainly wasn't extravagant. She didn't spend what she had on diamonds and flash handbags. She believed that you got what you paid for and that an investment in a coat that cost a little more would pay off in the long run. We are talking about a woman who could make a pair of shoes last several years here, so her theory was proven. She had aspirations for us as well. She wanted us to look good, even if the house we lived in had bare floorboards and a kitchen that was two decades out of date.

When I started Rise Park Junior School at the age of seven I was taken to London on the hunt for the perfect school coat. In previous years I had worn coats from George at Asda, but this particular year it was time for me to advance to another level. Mum took me to Selfridges, one of the most exclusive department stores in the country. I didn't know too much about brands and fashion when I was small but to me the place was magical. My eyes were wide with wonder as I was ushered through the grand halls of the store. It was packed with shoppers and the first thing that hit me when I walked through the doors was the smell of expensive perfume. It hung so heavy in the air it was almost like a drug. The crowds and noise seemed to pass by in slow motion as I tried to take it all in.

We headed to the children's department on a mission to find something that would make me stand out at my new school. I knew as soon as I saw it that I was meant to wear it. It was there, shining at me from a hanger on a rail, whispering, 'Buy me'. It was a satin Puffa jacket printed with a map of the North Pole and pictures of polar bears. It was white and silver and it had fur round the hood. Mum nodded approvingly as I took it off the rail and slipped it on. It was so warm it almost hugged me and when I wore it I felt like a million dollars. I looked like an Essex Eskimo! I had to have it and I was over the moon when Mum agreed to buy it for me. She must have caught the bug too because that same day she treated herself to a leather coat from Armani. It was the first designer item I ever remember her buying and it had an aura that made our family treat it with a kind of reverence. If we were out and someone mentioned her coat I would whisper to them, 'It's an Armani,' as if it were some amazing secret. I had no idea who or what Armani was but it sounded very important to me.

It was around that time that I first started to develop what would turn into a complicated relationship with food. Today, I know with the benefit of hindsight that I have been prone to comfort-eating during stressful periods in my life – more about that later. The association I have with comfort and food began back when I was a little girl, and especially when I would go on these shopping trips to London with Mum.

Throughout junior school those trips became increasingly common. I loved them. I looked forward so much to my dancing and singing and the inevitable trip to Oxford Street, Regent Street or Knightsbridge that would follow. I wasn't always bought things, but the one thing I could rely on was that there would be some kind of food treat in the afternoon.

'Come on Gem,' Mum would wink as we were wandering around Harrods, 'let's get an ice cream.' And we would head to the posh ice-cream parlour for a few scoops of decadence. In truth Mum couldn't afford much in the shops she liked to go in, but the one thing she could buy was a cone of ice cream or a bar of chocolate. During the summer holidays we would go to London three or four times a week. We didn't always have somewhere particular to go; we'd just hop on the tube and see where we ended up. That woman traipsed me up and down Oxford Street more times than I had hot dinners. And each time she would get me a little treat – of food. Then in the evening, when we got home after our fun day together, we would all go out for a meal. I have very lovely memories of those days and many of them involve food. I was happy and secure and I felt special.

Mum, of course, had no idea that her actions would trigger comfort-eating later in my life. She just wanted me to be happy and to feel loved, which I did. She in turn used giving treats to her children as a way of passing on the love she felt she'd missed out on as a child. And it was also a way for her to feel like she'd finally made a success of her life. It meant more to her to be able to give us the things she never had than anything else. She once told me that when she was a kid, a treat for her would be a sugar sandwich. So the fact that she could buy me an ice cream from Harrods made her feel great.

When I look back now it was madness how it all changed, how in the space of a few years I went from living in a modest house with no luxuries, toasting bread on a fork in front of a gas fire, to regular treats in Harrods, but I guess that was because my parents were living the Essex dream. We were a self-made family. Dad worked hard, he was ambitious and he put in the hours. His efforts were rewarded. Most of the families in Essex are self-made. The county is full of family businesses and grafters; people who take chances, who roll with the punches and who have self-belief.

At the start of another term Mum took me to the John Lewis flagship store on Oxford Street and bought me a navy blue cashmere coat. It was beautifully tailored and had a little split up the back hem that was lined with green material. The collar was trimmed with velvet. Each new year at school I would rock up with what we in Essex would call 'the nuts of a coat' (that means it was pretty special).

Mum's obsession with keeping me looking good and kitting me out in classy clothes reached fever pitch one summer when she read about a pair of shoes that Sarah Ferguson had bought for the two princesses, Eugenie and Beatrice. Mum saw the name of the shoemaker and had seen the shoes in a photograph in a magazine. She was determined to get a pair for me. I was going to have shoes fit for a princess. Mum set about finding the stockists of this particular make and style. I've long since forgotten what they were but I do remember that they were round-toed with dainty little buttons on them. Apparently a lot of the royal children wore them. I was dragged all over the south-east hunting for a pair. The irony was that although we were looking for a pair of royal appointed shoes, we drove round looking for them in Mum's car – a red Ford Escort estate – because Dad was still too careful with his money to splash out on anything nicer. He'd traded his own Orion in for a Ford Sierra. We'd pull up outside these ultra-posh shoe boutiques, me in my Selfridges coat, Mum in her Armani, and we'd climb out of a crappy car that was so bright it could be seen from space! People didn't know what to make of us. I dread to think what Dad thought about Mum's mission. He is still one of the most understated people you could ever meet.

Eventually, after we'd tried all of the shoe shops in Essex and most of the ones in London, we finally found a stockist about thirty miles away in Hertfordshire. It became Mum's favourite shoe shop and, while the other kids at school started each new term with a new pair of shoes from Clarks if they were lucky, I started with a pair by royal appointment.

Mum developed the same attitude to my dancewear. When I first signed up for dance classes she came along with me to the induction. We were shown round the studios by a lady called Jackie who ran the school and she explained all about the dance styles I would be learning. She also explained what I would need to wear.

'Gemma will need some Lycra dancing leggings,' she told Mum. 'Most of the mums get them from Romford Market. There's a stall there that does decent ones for about £10; they'll do – you don't need anything flash.'

I could tell by the way Mum looked that the thought of kitting me out in an outfit from the market troubled her. It may have only been a weekend dance school in a hall in Dagenham, but I was going to have the best Lycra money could buy. Mum set about researching where to get it from. She discovered that all the top dancers got their outfits from a historic theatrical costume shop called Borovick in Soho in London. That's where we headed and that's where I got my outfit from.

So there I was, kitted out in the best clothes money could buy, with shoes fit for royalty, and a head full of dreams that one day I would be a star. Mum filled me with self-belief; she was convinced I had the X factor. Dad was more reserved and laid back; he wouldn't care if I had a career in Greggs the baker as long as I was happy. I was an all-singing, all-dancing Essex princess and I left junior school looking forward to a bright future. What on earth could possibly go wrong?

CHAPTER FOUR

SCHOOL DAYS

'**W**e are an academic school. Students will be taught how to learn and how to achieve the best possible grades in the subjects which they take. But this is only one part of an outstanding and complete education. We believe that our approach must be holistic; that we must support the physical, moral and spiritual development of our girls.'

That was the mission statement from the Frances Bardsley Academy for Girls in Romford, the place where I was heading to spend my teenage years.

I sat in my bedroom on the Sunday night before my first day at big school contemplating my future. What would it be like at an all-girls' school? How much homework would I get? How many times a week would I do drama?

I carefully put my new books in the handmade leather satchel that Mum had bought for me from a shop in Covent Garden. My cashmere coat was hanging on the back of my bedroom door along with my new uniform, which consisted of a green skirt and blazer combo and a yellow blouse. The exercise books for my new subjects were covered, as requested by the school, in crisp plain brown paper. My name was written on the front of each. I had added a few words of my own, just to personalise them. *Gemma*

Collins: A Star is born, I wrote, and finished the design off with a few musical notes. I was ready to have my physique, my morality and my spirituality developed.

The following morning I met up with Vicky Rance at the entrance to the school. Much to my excitement, she'd got a place there too.

Mum dropped us off. As it was a special occasion, Dad let her use the Sierra so we didn't have to face the indignity of arriving for our first day in the bright red Escort. Vicky and I stood at the school entrance, hand in hand. I gave her hand a little squeeze and we walked through the wrought-iron gates into our new world. The school had a well-tended front courtyard. There was a pathway leading down the centre towards the front doors and lawns on either side, which were decorated with well-tended flower beds and rose-bushes. There were girls everywhere. The older pupils strolled in with confidence and the Year Sevens – the newbies – stuck out like sore thumbs. We were all in crisp, clean new uniforms and most looked around nervously, trying to blend in.

I don't remember ever being worried though. I had loved junior school and had made loads of friends there but I was excited about a new challenge. The acting and dancing lessons and the extra-curricular activities Mum lined up for me, together with the regular trips into the hustle and bustle of London, had instilled a confidence in me a lot of other girls my age didn't have. I never shied away from trying something new and as far as I was concerned a new school was just a bigger stage for me to act up on.

Thankfully Vicky was in the same class as me. We felt safe together and for the first few months we hung round together all day. We soon came to the attention of the wider pupil population because Vicky was a thin, tiny girl, thinner than Kate Moss, and growing into a very beautiful girl. By contrast, I was very tall, probably the tallest in the year, and was slim with long hair.

I had always towered above my peers and every Christmas at junior school had been given the part of the Angel Gabriel in the nativity play because I stood out. At secondary school I quickly earned the nickname Big Bird, after the character from the children's television show *Sesame Street*. I wasn't offended. I felt pleased that I was making an impression.

From the start I was outgoing and I soon made new friends. In my first year at secondary school I became friendly with a group of girls and we would hang out together in class and during break. There were the sisters Cassie and Louise Morgan, who I am still friends with today, and Laura Barber. The Morgan family and the Barber family were close, so the girls were a ready-made social unit when they started school. There was also Kelly, Liz, Hannah, Katie, Jenny and Sasha. We had our own little clique.

At the weekends the gang would head to Romford to hang out in the high street. We were all the same age and in those early teenage years we had started to become aware of our femininity and were getting interested in make-up and fashion. It was very important to be seen in the right things, from the clothes you wore to the lipstick you used. At the time, the must-have lippy of choice for any teenage girl around town in Romford was Rimmel Earth Star. The girls of Frances Bardsley must have used gallons of the stuff. If you turned up in class without a decent slick of Earth Star on your lips you were nobody. It wasn't pink, it was quite a nude, creamy shade very similar to MAC Blankety. It was popular with teenage girls because you could wear it at school and it didn't look as obvious as a brighter colour. I completed the look with a generous covering of Number 17 bronzing pearls, which I used to use before I discovered bronzer and started whacking that on instead.

I also started to follow fashion. I had the classy clothes from the top London stores but the more I hung round with my new friends, the more I wanted to wear what all the teenage girls were wearing. And in the early nineties that meant brands like Naf Naf and LA Gear. Mum tried to fob me off with Benetton. She went through a Benetton phase and tried to dress me from head to toe in it, but I just wanted to wear what my friends were wearing. Naf Naf at the time was really exclusive and I was always on at my mum to get me new stuff. Eventually she gave in and when I needed a new tracksuit I was treated to a bright red one with a huge multi-coloured Naf Naf logo across the back. I finished the look off with a pair of LA Gear trainers. There was competition among us girls to see who could have the best stuff; who could have the most trainers or the most Naf Naf gear. I even had a Naf Naf pencil case at one point. It was never nasty though and we all realised how lucky we were. We would also challenge each other about our favourite boybands. I loved Take That, I lived and breathed them. Robbie was my favourite. He ticked all the boxes for me: he was wild, he was risky. Vicky on the other hand was into East 17 and we used to have heated debates about who was the best.

I was still singing and dancing and a real extrovert; my confidence allowed me to be one of the school's biggest performers. In assembly we would have to stand up and sing hymns and halfway through I would bust out into my favourite Madonna number.

'Hey girls, do you believe in love?' I would sing. My mates would crack up laughing and we'd all get in trouble. Singing 'Morning Has Broken' wasn't my style. But it was all good fun and although I was sometimes marked out as a show-off, the teachers knew I wasn't a troublemaker and when reports of my disruptions did reach Mum via parents evening, she just put it down to my acting talent and argued that it should be encouraged, rather than suppressed.

When I was about fourteen Mum decided that there was enough money in the household budget to send me to one of the country's most famous acting schools, the Sylvia Young Theatre School. I went there for Saturday lessons. It was the school that many of the cast of *EastEnders* had attended, from Danniella Westbrook to Adam Woodyatt and Dean Gaffney, and it had also produced pop stars such as Lee Ryan from Blue and Amy Winehouse. Mum believed that in order to give myself the best possible chance of stardom, I needed the best education money could buy. And it was very handy for her because the school was in central London, so she could drop me off on a Saturday morning and then go into town and go shopping.

Normally I was very confident and welcomed new situations, but I never felt settled at Sylvia Young. I didn't know anyone there and if I am honest I only agreed to go to please Mum. I knew she was only doing it because she wanted the best for me and she wanted me to be the best I could be, but I didn't enjoy the feeling of being left alone in London. I liked the local dance school I was at, the Everett Dance Academy. I had been going there for several years, I had friends there, it was a social thing for me. Sylvia Young was a different league. It was serious.

I also started having elocution lessons with a lady called Cherry Miller who lived in a big house in South Woodford, because Mum believed that if I was going to be an actor I needed to be good at speaking posh. She got a little overambitious with it all. Throughout the week I ended up having extra singing lessons, extra dancing lessons, extra acting lessons and learning to speak in different accents. I was a teenager and basically there were times when I felt I just wanted to hang out on Romford High Street with my friends or go to the cinema with them, but Mum kept me busy all the time and most weekends the nearest I got to hanging out on the high street was when I got taken to Miss Selfridge and treated to a blow-dry in the salon there.

It felt like I was waiting for stardom to find me and eventually, when I was fourteen, all that preparation paid off.

I heard Mum gasp from the lounge, where she was sitting reading the paper.

'They are auditioning for parts in *The Sound of Music*, you have to go Gem,' she called out excitedly.

I ran in to look at the small ad in the local paper. They wanted singers and dancers for various parts in a production of the play that was being staged in the Queen's Theatre, Hornchurch; a glass and concrete venue not too far from where we lived.

There was no debating, I was as excited as Mum and as the time of the auditions drew nearer we both became increasingly animated about what it would be like when I got the part. It didn't dawn on us that I might not be successful. Mum loved the theatre. She would often go to the Queen's and sit in the cafe there and have a cuppa. She liked the feel of the place.

On the day of the audition Dad took me – Mum was either busy or too nervous to watch me. The auditions were being held in the main auditorium and there were loads of aspiring actors and dancers there, all milling around, singing and generally showing off. I waited until it was my turn and bounded on stage with as much confidence as I could muster. It was like being on *Britain's Got Talent*. There was a panel of three people in front of me, who I assumed were the directors and choreographers. I was up for the part of one of the nuns. I was tall enough to pass off as an adult and I'd also be wearing a habit, so the audience wouldn't notice how young I was.

Dad was sitting in a seat behind the panel willing me on.

A lady sitting in front of me introduced herself and asked me to perform a dance move 'that would ensure I stand out from all the other hopefuls'.

I ran across the stage dramatically and leapt in the air, kicking my legs as if I was in the movie *Fame*. I did a little routine I had been practising and then it was over. The lady thanked me and I walked off stage towards Dad. As I got near him I whispered: 'I nailed it.' I had been dancing long enough to know I'd put in a good performance.

The lady overheard me, turned around and scolded: 'Don't be too sure my dear.'

My heart sank a little and we were told to wait with the others in a holding area outside. It was a nerve-shredding thirty minutes before the panel came out and read the names of the successful candidates.

When I heard my name I let out a triumphant shriek and Dad hugged me. I was going to be a theatre star!

I loved being in that production. It ran for a month and I did most nights, plus matinees at the weekend. I even got paid £25 a week. Mum used to pick me up from school and take me to the theatre, where she'd proudly watch most of my performances.

Over the years she made sure I entered plenty of singing and dancing competitions. I won the south-east England song and dance championships after belting out a rendition of '42nd Street' and I was picked to represent England in a show in the Czech Republic.

It was my first big foreign assignment and I was chosen along with several other people from the Theatretrain Academy. Mum would never have let me go on my own so she came along too. I had my own number to perform. The theme was Great Britain and I was going to sing Vera Lynn's wartime classic 'We'll Meet Again' in front of a Czech audience.

The show itself was great. I got a real buzz from the applause I got from the audience after my solo. But the accommodation we were shown to after was horrific. The group I was with had been booked into a hostel just outside Prague and to say it was basic was an understatement. I had never seen anything like it. The walls were grey, bare bulbs hung from the ceilings, the communal shower facilities were cold, dank and dark and the beds we were supposed to sleep on were old and covered by threadbare mattresses and old dusty blankets. I took one look at the place and started crying. I remember feeling very ill, depressed and scared. I had never seen a hostel like it before. It was bad. Even the people in it looked bad; they were grey. Mum was too shocked to speak. I begged her to ring Dad. I couldn't stay there. It was awful.

From the UK, Dad saved the day. He managed to find a hotel for us in Prague and used his credit card to book a room. I couldn't get out the hostel fast enough and although it meant leaving my fellow cast members, I didn't care. I just wanted warm water and a soft bed. The hotel we went to was like a palace. We had a room with a huge king-size bed and big, fluffy white feather pillows. We ordered room service and had a restful night's sleep.

While Mum was happy to accompany me to acting and singing assignments, she was less willing to allow me to go on school trips. She even didn't want me to get the bus to school on my own and for several years insisted on driving me every day. It wasn't that she didn't want me to go and enjoy myself; she was just petrified something might happen to me. Her background obviously came into it; having been abandoned as a kid herself, she felt she had a right of duty to protect me and look after me. She believed the teachers were not responsible enough. The only trip I was ever allowed to go on was to Ypres in Belgium and I had to really push her to let me go. I was thirteen and it was arranged to tie in with our history curriculum. At the time we were learning about the First World War and on the trip we would visit some of the battlegrounds in the area.

When the day of the trip came, Mum waved me off on the coach and I could see the look of fear in her face. I was too excited to worry about it though. The school had limited our spending money to £10, which was supposed to last a couple of days, but Dad slipped me £30. I had a new coat (yes, another one) and although I'd just wanted a £10 Puffa jacket from the market, Mum insisted on taking me to Miss Selfridge to get me a new outfit. There was also a brand called Portofino that was popular at the time – it was a little like Naf Naf – and I bought a new Portofino pencil case with matching pens and pencils.

I felt really grown-up as I set off to see the war trenches and spent a couple of fun-filled days trudging around war graves in Belgium and northern France with my friends. There was a song out at the time by the Fugees called 'Ready Or Not' that used a sample from a song by Enya, 'Boadicea'. It was a spooky, atmospheric piece of music and the school chose it as the theme to a video of the trip that we all made. I got a part presenting it and every time I hear that music today it makes me smile and cringe a little. I was on the video like a teenage Kate Adie in a navy tracksuit, wearing a tin hat, reporting on a war that had been over decades ago.

A year or so later I persuaded my parents to allow me to go on another trip, this time skiing in the Alps. My friends were all going and I knew it would be fun. Dad paid the £250 deposit. One day, as it was coming close to the time when the balance needed to be paid, I was sitting watching the news with Mum and an item came on which I knew would strike fear into her heart. It was a tragic story about some children who had been on a school trip and had been in an accident. One of them had died. His weeping mum was on the TV, distraught at her loss.

When the report was over the room was silent. I knew exactly what was going through Mum's mind. After a couple of minutes she turned and looked at me.

'Are you sure you want to go skiing?' she asked. 'You've never been before. I don't think you will enjoy it.'

Over the following days I started to wonder whether going was such a good idea after all. She was right: I'd never been skiing, I wasn't sure if it was the type of thing I'd enjoy. In some lessons I sat next to a girl who suffered from a condition called goitre. It made her neck look fat, as though she had swallowed a rubber ring. She was a lovely girl and she took stick from some of the other pupils. She had wanted to go on the trip but her family hadn't been able to afford it. I decided I was going to do something decent. I told my parents that I didn't want to go and that as Dad was going to lose his deposit anyway, there was someone who could use it. Dad wasn't too happy about losing the money but I reckon he felt it was worth it if they didn't have to worry about me breaking my leg on the piste any more. The next time I saw the girl at school I made an excuse that I had a dancing competition and told her that if she wanted it she could have my deposit. I didn't want to make a big deal of it and she was overjoyed. Her parents scraped the rest of the money together and she went on the trip in my place.

Although I look back now and realise that my parents were extremely protective, I never felt that I was missing out – quite the opposite. I have lovely childhood memories. To me it just felt as if Mum and Dad loved me so much and they were scared that something was going to happen to me. Years later when I started working in London, Mum would tell me not to stand too close to the platform on the Underground and still today when I travel around London, the minute I stand on a tube platform I can hear her dulcet tones in my head: 'Do not stand on the edge of that platform Gemma, someone might push you.' She put the fear of God into me. She always taught me to keep my bag close and to be astute, to never to open my purse in front of people and to be on my guard. She always had a thing when I was a teenager about making sure I wore clean underwear. I always hear my mum in the back of my head saying 'Do not leave the house with dirty knickers on' – as if I would. I asked her why and she said because if anything ever happened to me and I needed medical attention at least I would be wearing clean pants!

The one thing my parents didn't have to worry about was boys. When I started secondary school and for a few years after, I just wasn't interested. I was too engrossed in my singing and dancing. Being at an all-girls' school helped. There wasn't the day-to-day temptation, although there was a boys' school just down the road, which, as they got older, many of the girls at Frances Bardsley seemed to be drawn to.

I loved Robbie Williams and I could appreciate a pop hunk as much as the next girl but when it came to boys my age, I didn't fancy them and I couldn't care less about them. My friends started to have flirtations with boys and I was pleased for them but it just never appealed to me. I was too busy.

My aversion to boys wasn't a two-way street however and boys from the neighbouring school had started to take an interest in me. I was slim and good-looking. I was never aware of it, though, because I came from a family that never talked about people's looks. We took people as they were. I wasn't obsessed with how I looked and I didn't think looks were the be-all and end-all. I made decisions about people based on their personalities and whether they made me laugh.

I was never allowed to dress provocatively – I had to be covered up. I was never encouraged to look sexy. I was naive about my body. When I was thirteen Mum told me I needed a bra and I was mortified. It was embarrassing. My first cup size was a 32AA because there was nothing there. Mum took me to Marks & Spencer to get measured and bought me three starter bras. I wore one home and when I got back I went straight to my room, took it off and put a vest on instead.

One boy who took a shine to me was Dean Mascoll. He had been on the bus on the rare occasions I was allowed to ride it home. He had tried talking to me in the giggly way boys did and I quite liked him, but I played it cool because I didn't want to give him the wrong impression. Unbeknown to me, he took Kelly Puckett aside one day and asked her for my phone number, which she willingly gave out.

I was at home watching television when the phone rang.

'I'll get it,' Mum called and walked into the hall to answer the call.

I heard snatches of the strained conversation through the door.

'Who is this?' she asked. 'OK, I'll get her.'

Mum called me.

'It's a boy for you, Gemma,' she said.

I picked up the phone and Dean was on the other end of the line, laughing nervously.

'Hi Gemma,' he said. 'Kelly gave me your number.' He tried to strike up a conversation. We talked awkwardly. He asked if I'd be on the bus the next day.

'No,' I answered plainly. There was a pause. Dean didn't know what else to say.

'Er, oh, OK. Bye.' He hung up. Part of me was secretly pleased he had called, the other part was perplexed. What did he want?

I walked back in the lounge and Mum looked at me.

'Who was that?' she asked.

'A boy called Dean,' I replied.

'How did he get your number?'

'Kelly gave it to him.'

Mum was not happy.

'She shouldn't be giving out our number to strangers,' she frowned. She thought about it for a few moments and then got up.

'That is out of order,' she said. 'I'm going to call Kelly's mum.'

'But Mum ...' I pleaded. I knew what would happen. I'd be a laughing stock the next day at school because my mum didn't want me talking to boys.

Mum made the call. I cringed as I heard her tell Mrs Puckett that under no circumstances was her daughter allowed to give our telephone number out again.

'I do not want my Gemma mixing with boys, I want my Gemma to concentrate on her dancing, her singing, her acting and her school work,' she said. I almost died of embarrassment and the next day I had to endure the jokes and giggling after Kelly told everyone how my strict parents wouldn't let me talk to boys.

I had a proper date when I was thirteen. It was only a fleeting, innocent relationship but I class Lee as my first boyfriend. I met him through Vicky, who by that time had blossomed into a very good-looking girl who always pulled the boys. She was going out with a guy called Wesley and I met Lee, his mate, through them. We met one rare Saturday when I wasn't at Sylvia Young and had been allowed out into Romford. Wesley and Lee were in the market and while Vicky was flirting with Wesley I got talking to

Lee. He was very good-looking. He did judo. He was very good at it but had sustained a terrible injury to his head when he was younger and had needed metal plates in his skull to reconstruct it, although you couldn't tell. He was tall with light brown hair cut into the curtains style that everyone had in the nineties. He was a very kind soul with a twinkle in his eyes and he made me laugh. When he asked me to go round his house for a Chinese takeaway and to watch a film I had butterflies in my tummy.

'I'll have to ask my parents,' I answered nervously.

That evening I spoke to my mum and dad and at first they said they didn't think I was ready for a boyfriend. But they could see I was excited and in their hearts they knew they couldn't keep me young for ever. They realised the best they could do was try to control the situation and minimise the risks. They reluctantly agreed, but stipulated that I had to have dinner with Lee's parents as well as him and stated that under no circumstances was I allowed to go up to his bedroom.

I called Lee excitedly to tell him I was allowed to go round to his house and we arranged the date for the following Saturday.

That week seemed to take an age to pass and all I could think about was my upcoming date. I planned in my head what I was going to wear; jeans and a top from Miss Selfridge, I decided, and I started getting ready with plenty of time to spare. I slicked on my Rimmel Earth Star and sung along to the Tina Arena song 'Chains', which was a big hit at the time.

Dad drove me to Lee's house in Rise Park. I got there at 7.30 p.m. and Dad said he would be back at 10.30 p.m. on the dot to pick me up and take me home.

The date was uneventful. Lee and I had a Chinese takeaway with his parents and then we all sat down together to watch a movie. I can't remember what it was. There was no big love affair with Lee but it was nice having a little dinner date, and although he wasn't my boyfriend for long nevertheless we went on to be friends. I don't know what he is doing now.

As I progressed through school my circle of friends grew. Vicky was always my closest pal but I was a social floater and had lots of different friends in different groups. I was an all-rounder and I was happy. But life started to change when I was fourteen and hormones started to rage in the girls at school. People started bickering and we all found different interests. We started to drift apart.

I was still friendly with Laura. At school she was the first person I remember going on a diet, even though she was never big, and she'd sometimes end up giving me her sandwiches at lunch. Perhaps that was what swayed it!

Meeting Louise Morgan was the best thing about that school and I am still very close with her; she is like a sister to me. I'll never forget when I first saw her in the corridor and thought she was beautiful. I am very lucky to have her in my life today.

But otherwise my friends started to drift apart and I began to lose touch with so many people. It was really sad. Around that time I felt that there was a real change in the atmosphere of the school. Girls who were previously my friends started to blank me and others started to make snide comments. I was sitting on the bus once minding my own business when a group of older girls I vaguely knew began singing the words to the Divinyls song 'I Touch Myself'.

'I love myself,' they laughed. I knew the words were directed at me because of my singing and dancing ambitions and my confidence. I felt my cheeks flush hot with embarrassment. I started to worry every day about going to school, not that I would have let anyone know about it.

I was taunted for being outgoing and for being who I was. Outside of school I would walk past certain gangs of girls and I could feel them staring at me, I could sense their hostility and hear them muttering things under their breath. I hated it. My confidence began to ebb away. I was scared to be myself in case it invited abuse. In a few short months it got to the point where I started to feel sick at the thought of going to school; not because I was scared someone was going to hit me, but because I didn't like all the arguing and the upheaval. While on the outside I was an outgoing, gregarious girl who appeared to want to be the centre of attention, underneath there was and always has been shyness and a naivety about me. I would not let most people see that, though; only the people who really know me see that side. People have always misunderstood me to a large degree. Underneath it all I have always been ultra-sensitive and back then I felt like my life was spinning out of control.

CHAPTER FIVE

BULLIED AND BEATEN, BUT NOT OUT

The highlight of the school social calendar was the local underage disco. There were two held in nightclubs nearby for under-eighteens, both in Romford – one was at a club called Ritzy, the other was at Hollywood's. They were probably meant for students a little older than the thirteen-year-old clientele who actually attended them, because they were held on weeknights and went on until midnight, which was late to be out on a school night for a first or second-year student. I started going to them when I was thirteen and a half and there were plenty of girls and boys my age who went too and stayed until the end. At midnight, concerned parents would line up in their cars outside waiting to pick up their kids. In school you always knew when there had been an underage disco because half the kids would be falling asleep at their desks!

We used to go to the underage disco nights in a big group, all of us dressed up in club wear and glowing with bronzer. I continued to go with Laura and Vicky after the group fell apart.

I was never a teen drinker and they never sold alcohol at the under-eighteen nights anyway. From my early teens I was allowed a drink socially at the dinner table and I think that's why I've never been a binge drinker. I looked old enough to get served in some pubs from the age of fourteen. As a teenager in Essex you got to know the pubs where you could get served. The most popular at the time was the Spencers Arms in Hornchurch where you could sometimes pull the wool over their eyes and get served. It used to be a bit of a dive back then but I was allowed to go there and do karaoke on Sundays as long as I was home before 10 p.m. The clientele consisted of kids from families who had money, so everyone would get dressed up to go and try to outdo each other. I used to have a few Archers and lemonades, but getting pissed was never my thing.

At school there always seemed to be tit for tat arguments and feuds going on and it became hard to keep track of them as rows between different cliques of girls escalated. I didn't know who liked me and who didn't any more. It had really started to get me down.

Mum sensed that there were problems. I'd get home and she could tell that I was unhappy.

'What's the matter Gem?' she asked once.

'It's a nightmare, Mum,' I told her. 'Everyone has fallen out. Everyone is arguing. I can't take it any more.'

I really couldn't. I locked away most of my feelings because I didn't want to worry anyone else with them but I was becoming increasingly down and anxious. My confidence was suffering. I just wanted to enjoy school and have fun but every day I would wake up worried that I'd be the subject of snide remarks and wondering who would fall out with who next.

One Wednesday I resolved to cheer myself up with a night out in Ritzy. The previous Saturday I had treated myself to a snake-skin-effect PVC jacket from Miss Selfridge and I was looking for an excuse to wear it out. Dad agreed that I could go as long as I was home and in bed by midnight. All the other kids went and he knew that allowing me a little freedom would stop me sneaking off on my own. He agreed to take me and Laura and so I finished school, went home, finished off my homework and started to get ready. I complemented the jacket with a tight short dress and a pair of patent-leather high-heeled shoes. I felt the Don when I stepped out my front door, and ignored Dad's remarks about the length of my dress and the height of my heels!

At first I was apprehensive. Would any of the girls I had fallen out with be there? Laura and I walked in bravely and after a while we began to relax and hit the dance floor for a boogie. For the first time in weeks I started to relax and let my hair down. Laura went off to get a drink and that's when it happened.

I didn't see the girl approach; I just felt the blow. She walked up to me from the side and landed a stinging punch on the bridge of my nose. She caught me square on with her knuckles and I staggered backwards in shock, instinctively holding my hands up to protect my face. I was dazed. Through my fingers I saw the girl stoop down and pick up my bag, which I had been dancing round and which contained my money and door keys. She ran off into the crowd before I could even try to stop her.

I was in shock. I stood there shaking, trying to work out what had just happened. Dad had given me £30 for the night and as well as that, the bag contained a new purse from Next that I had treated myself to. I could feel my eye begin to swell and it was pulsing with pain. The club was packed, people were looking at me and asking if I was OK but I felt alone, scared and exposed. All my life my parents had taken great pains to shield me and protect me and suddenly I was experiencing real life. I didn't like it at all.

I didn't want to hang around and I was too scared to go off and look for Laura. I had no money: I'd have to use the public phone in the reception area. I ran off to it through the crowd and made a reverse-charge call home. It was 10 p.m. and when Dad answered I could hear the concern in his voice.

I was crying.

'Can you come and pick me up please Dad?' I sobbed. 'Someone has just hit me.'

'Are you OK Gemma, are you in any danger?' he asked urgently.

I told him I was OK and that I was with Laura. He told me to go and wait outside and that he would be there within ten minutes.

I left the club without Laura and stood shaking in the cold. I have never been so relieved to see a Ford than when I saw him race down Romford High Street in his car. He was like a knight in shining armour. I got in the passenger seat and he hugged me. He looked suicidal. All his life he'd looked after me and I guess he felt now that he had let me down because he wasn't there. He couldn't believe that someone had done that to me. I was in so much pain. By that time my eye was a puffy, red mess. Dad wanted to go back inside the club and find the girl who had hit me but I knew it was related to all the fallings-out at school and I knew that it would only escalate matters if I started to make a fuss. I tried to play it down.

When I got home Mum was awake. She made me a sweet cup of tea and got an ice pack to press on my eye. Around half an hour later Laura's mum pulled up at the house and rapped on the door.

She wanted to know what had happened and to check that I was OK. I was exhausted and when she'd left I fell into bed and slept.

The following morning when I went down to the kitchen for breakfast, Mum and Dad were sitting at the table, stony-faced. My eye had closed over and the bruising was coming out. It was blue, red and angry. They recoiled a little when they saw me. Mum shook her head.

'This is out of hand now, we don't think being in that all-girls' school is good for you,' she said. It was the first time she had mooted the idea of me moving school. It hadn't occurred to me that I could. I'd assumed I would just have to keep my head down until it all died down.

'It's fine Mum, honestly,' I assured her. 'It'll sort itself out.' I didn't want them to worry for me, even though I wasn't really confident that things would settle down.

After the attack my anxiety got ten times worse. I got sick in my stomach. Some mornings I would be doubled up in pain from the churning in my belly. It got so bad I could never go to the toilet in school. I used to get Mum to pick me up and take me home in my lunch hour so I could poo. I wonder what a psychoanalyst would say about that? I also didn't like the tracing-paper style toilet roll there, so Mum would put a double deluxe roll of Andrex in my schoolbag just in case I ever got caught short.

All my life Mum had told me not to be nervous and to walk tall. 'When you walk in a room, walk in like you own it,' she would say. But deep down, under the bravado I was shy, and now the safe bubble I had been living in had burst. I was scared. I fronted it out but inside I was a mess. I had always been popular – sometimes it was exhausting because I was always invited to parties – but suddenly I realised my outgoing personality and my zest for life were rubbing people up the wrong way and singling me out for bullying.

I didn't want to go to school any more and I started to bunk off. I used to get ready as normal, put on my uniform, pack my bag and pretend to my mum I was going. I was older now and allowed to make my own way to classes in the morning. But rather than get on the bus to Frances Bardsley, I would get on the 296 bus to Ilford and go to see my friend Susie. She was a friend from drama classes. She went to the Italia Conti School, a famous stage school similar to Sylvia Young. She was having trouble there and so we found comfort in each other. She was the only person who I truly opened up to about my feelings. I used to go to her house and all we did all day was sing and dance. Then, when it got to 2.30 p.m. I'd go back home and pretend I had been at school all day. I wasn't nervous about bunking off. It was exciting and it was easy to pull the wool over Mum's eyes. The school never cottoned on because I forged letters to say I had been sick.

On the days I did go to school Vicky agreed to accompany me on the bus to look out for me. She was a great friend, she always has been, and I had to lean on her for support. To try and calm my nerves I would play positive, happy music to keep my mind off what was happening. It was as though each morning I had to put on a suit of armour.

Dad had his own practical solution to the problem. He got me self-defence lessons. He'd been so traumatised by seeing me after the attack that he wanted to make sure if it happened again I could look after myself. I used to go to the Roller Bowl Gym in Collier

Row with him and there was a guy there called Blue. He was very good-looking. Basically, he was the first guy who properly turned my head after Robbie Williams. He was a bit of a hunk was Blue and he was into martial arts. Dad had a word with him, told him that I was being picked on and asked him to come round to the house and show me some moves. I wasn't sure if it was the right way to tackle the situation. I'm not a violent person and I couldn't hit anyone to save my life. But I went along with the plan and the following Saturday morning before I went to Sylvia Young, Blue turned up in his tight white vest and sweatpants to teach me how to look after myself. He brought a selection of pads and gloves to use and for an hour I bounced around the back garden with him, throwing wild punches in his direction. The lessons lasted several weeks but learning to fight wasn't me. I went through the motions to please Dad but I got up one Saturday morning and decided to be honest with him.

'I don't want to do this any more, it's just not me. I don't want to have to feel that I need to learn self-defence,' I told him. In my logic, by learning how to fight back, I was accepting that the bullies had won.

In the end fate intervened. It started with a friend of mine and a nasty case of the lurgy. I was in Year Ten and was hanging around with this girl. She was always coughing and so when she went off ill for a couple of weeks no one thought anything of it. We assumed it was one of the regular bouts of sniffles she suffered from. But she had contracted glandular fever, a very nasty viral infection of the glands in the neck that leads to a sore throat, swollen neck and extreme tiredness. It can lead to ME, a chronic fatigue condition that leaves sufferers unable to do anything. It is not a pleasant condition to have and it stays in your system for ages. She did go on to develop ME and was poorly for a long time.

Anyway, a week or so after my friend disappeared from school, I started to get a scratchy throat and became extremely tired. I was kept off school and initially Mum thought it was a psychosomatic reaction to the problems I was having. It wasn't however, and I soon developed a fever and all the other symptoms of glandular fever. I had blood tests and the GP confirmed that I had caught the virus. It was an awful illness. I would struggle to get up in the morning and feel drained and tired. Some days I would swing between being exhausted and full of energy. One minute I barely had enough energy to walk and the next I'd be up and prancing around in the living room. Given what was going on in school I didn't need a great deal of encouragement to stay at home. I'm not saying it was pleasant but on the days when I felt OK I would realise that being off was a result. I am a fighter and a strong girl but the fever hit me hard. With my final year at school and GCSEs approaching I was sent work to do. The illness took ages to clear up. At its worst I was out for days and couldn't move. I would struggle down to the sofa in the morning and Mum would feed me chicken soup to try and keep my dwindling energy levels up. I would start to get better and then the illness would take me down again. It was frustrating and tiring. The virus stays with you for years and throughout my later teen years, whenever I got run down or stressed, I would get days when it came back and left me feeling fatigued. There is nothing you can take for it except medication to ease the symptoms and it took six weeks for me to recover enough to get back to school. By the time I returned it was a few days before the end of summer term and something had changed inside me. Before I got ill I'd faced going to school with grim inevitability. I accepted it was what I had to do and that I had to crack on and get through it. I didn't want the bullies to beat me so I'd showed a brave face to the world, even though inside I was scared and anxious.

When I eventually went back after the glandular fever, even though the friends I did have there were pleased to see me, I felt I no longer belonged. I could feel a change in the energy of the place. I deeply questioned why I was going. It was making me miserable and what was the point of being somewhere that made me unhappy? On my first day back I walked down the rose-bush-bordered path to the entrance and I was crying inside. Mum had sensed my anxiety in the run-up to my return and she told me, 'Gemma you haven't got to go to that school any more. If you don't want to go, we can find another school for you'. With her voice ringing in my ears I decided that I was leaving Frances Bardsley. It was a fateful decision that would lead me to becoming a TV star many years later. The following day I told Mum I wanted to leave and, as the summer holidays were approaching, we went to see the head and I never went back.

The day I walked down that path for the final time was such a relief. I was free. The knots that I used to get in my stomach every day when I had to go to that school started to unravel.

CHAPTER SIX

IN THE PRIVATES

was ready for a new start. The summer holidays came and my parents set about finding me a new place to spend my final school year. By then Dad's business was flying; he had started a new company called Unisystems Freight and money was coming in – and they decided that my last year would be spent at private school. I liked the idea. They found a school nearby in Hornchurch called Raphael Independent School. I'm not sure what the fees were at the time but now they charge £2600 a term so I imagine it set Dad back a few quid.

An interview with the headmaster was arranged and Mum set about the important business of preparing me. She coached me and sorted out an outfit that she hoped would show me to be an ideal private-school pupil. It was from Warehouse, my favourite shop at the time, and comprised a smart blazer and understated mint-green dress. I looked the part.

'Remember to speak nicely Gem,' she advised. 'Pull out all the stops and impress.'

On the day of the interview Dad put on his best suit and Mum went to the salon, had her hair done, and got dolled up. We drove there in the red Escort but parked it round the corner out of sight.

The first thing that struck me about Raphael was the size: it was small; much smaller than Frances Bardsley. You couldn't just walk in. You had to buzz a private intercom. We were invited in by one of the receptionists and shown to the head's office. The main corridor was carpeted. It felt very calm, safe and cosy. I got a good feeling about it. The classes were small, only about ten pupils per class.

During the interview I called on my elocution lesson experience and spoke in a fake posh accent. The head's name was Mr Malicka. I told him about my interests and why I wanted to attend his school and Dad explained the problems I'd had at Frances Bardsley. Mr Malicka nodded in an understanding way and explained that at Raphael good behaviour, mutual respect and cooperation were valued.

'We believe that each pupil is a unique individual who has the right to learn at school in a secure and structured environment,' he said.

Mum took great pains to tell him about my love of drama.

'Gemma is very good at drama, encourage her with her drama, she'll be famous one day,' she said. At the end of the interview Mr Malicka sat back in his chair, looked me in the eyes and told me that he would accept me into his school. I was relieved and happy. I felt like I'd passed the test, although when I look back now I realise the test was mostly about my dad's ability to pay the fees, rather than my academic ability.

After the interview we were given a tour of the school. It felt homely and I knew I would fit in. I even knew a couple of the pupils.

A few weeks later the new term started. On my first day I proudly put on my new burgundy blazer and was actually looking forward to the experience. There were no nerves. It felt right and when I arrived in class I felt very safe.

I settled in quickly and although I missed my friends from the other school I met a boy who remembered me from junior school and he showed me round. His name was Matthew Reilly and I still see him out and about in Essex now. He always says that he remembers me from school because I used to nick the Mars Bars from his lunchbox!

The differences between private school and state school were massive. Basically the pupils and teachers at Raphael had a bit more class about them. There was a whole different vibe there, the kids were nicer and I felt protected. You could tell they were better off. The cars dropping them off in the morning were Mercedes and Range Rovers. They dressed better: they had the latest gear, their bags and coats were designer and my wardrobe fitted in. I didn't feel out of place.

Before my first day, Mum and Dad had taken me to a shop in Romford called Choice. It was a high-end school shop for rich kids. I needed a new pair of school shoes and at the time the big brand was Patrick Cox. If you went to private school you needed a pair of Patrick Cox shoes and so I pestered Dad to buy me them.

'You get what you pay for Dad, they'll last,' I told him, reciting his mantra back at him. 'A pair of Clarks will set you back at least £40 and these will last longer. Look at it as an investment.'

As a man who made one pair of shoes last three years he couldn't disagree and reluctantly he agreed to pay £110 for them. He moaned about it for weeks but that was the hidden cost of a private education.

Over the following months many of my other friendships fizzled out. I lost contact with Laura, but later in life I re-established my relationships with her, Louise and Cassie and we are now great friends. I've always been a believer in moving on from the past. I still saw Vicky all the time though.

I found it refreshing to be at a mixed school even though I still wasn't that bothered about boys. It made the place feel different to what I had become used to; it was a different environment, it didn't feel as competitive or as bitchy.

The staff were very nurturing of my personality and I suppose that's where I felt the happiest because they understood me as a person. The school was very good at identifying pupils' talents and nurturing their qualities. I discovered there that I was good at art and the staff pushed me at it and encouraged me to achieve my potential. One of my pieces was entered in a local art competition in Havering and I won in my category. It was a collage and I was invited to an awards ceremony to pick up the prize but when we set off to the ceremony Mum was running late and I missed it. I did get another mention in the *Romford Recorder* though.

I started to relax. The troubles of the past were becoming a distant memory. It felt as if a weight had been lifted from my shoulders and the confidence that had been zapped from me over the preceding year began to return. The old Gemma was back! I started to go to underage Hollywood's every Tuesday night and saved up my pocket money and bought myself some Gucci sunglasses, which I wore to school every day.

After a night clubbing I'd inevitably arrive late and have to buzz the intercom to be let in. I got a bit of a reputation for being a latecomer.

'Gemma, it's half nine, you were supposed to be here at 8.30,' the receptionist would scold.

I'd make random excuses.

'I'm sorry but my cat got run over,' or 'The bus broke down.' In the end I just admitted that I had been at underage Hollywood's.

'It's my last year, I'm leaving soon, let me off,' I'd ask. And because you are a fee-paying pupil and a customer as well as a student they gave me a bit of leeway.

My whole attitude changed and the teachers encouraged it. I was happy and enthusiastic. I would get a little cheeky with them but never in a nasty way and they took it with good humour. I started wearing make-up to school and graduated from Rimmel to Clinique and Clarins, which was a real treat. I loved a bit of blusher and one day the French teacher, who would come to my house once a week to give me extra lessons and so knew a little about my history at Frances Bardsley, pulled me aside.

'Gemma you are only young, you don't need to be wearing make-up to school,' she said.

'But it makes me feel better Mrs Knowles,' I told her.

Another teacher I really got on well with was Mrs Francis. She was unusual because she had six toes. She told us about them and we'd always try and sneak a peek when she wore sandals. We had closer relationships with the teachers at Raphael than at state school and Mrs Francis had a crazy boyfriend who would often hire a minibus at the weekend and take groups of older pupils for nights out to London.

One morning when I was late I ran into the mum of one of the children at school. His name was TJ and she was Hazel. We got chatting and although she was older than me (and very glam; I remember her lipstick was peachy-orange with a shimmer and she smelled very expensive – she wore Obsession by Calvin Klein) we hit it off and each morning we'd run into each other and chat. I discovered that her husband ran a nearby garden centre, the Bedfords Road Nursery, and that he was in business with the family of another pupil at the school, a girl younger than me called Amy Childs. Through Hazel I met Amy's mum, Julie. Amy also had a cousin, Harry Derbidge. Hazel was a real laugh, a lovely character and I warmed to her immediately. She took to me too and over time started inviting me to family events where I got to know Julie, Amy and Harry.

Over the years Hazel became like a second mum to me. She was there through some of the darkest times of my life. She had glamorous parties in her house and, because the parents at the school were tight-knit, the Childs family were often there. When I first met them socially at a party I had the same feeling about Amy that my mum used to get about me.

'She's going to be famous one day, Julie,' I told her mum. Even then when she was a young teenager it was obvious she had something about her that made her different. And she had a lovely innocence.

'She is like a model, Julie, you've got to encourage her,' I said. She reminded me of a young Katie Price, before Katie had surgery. She was beautiful, funny and naive. She had everything going for her. Harry and Amy were not normal kids, they were destined for stardom, they stood out from everyone else.

I never realised at the time but meeting Hazel, and subsequently Julie Childs, would change my life for ever. I'm jumping the gun a little here but it was through Julie that I got invited to be in *TOWIE*. So even back then when I was approaching my sixteenth birthday it was all interconnected. It has left me with the belief that everything in life happens for a reason, and I look back now and I don't have any hang-ups about the bullying because it helped make me who I am and got me to where I am today.

It seemed like I had only been at Raphael for a short period when the time came to leave. Before exams we were allowed time off for study leave and the day we left depended on what day our final exams were. My last one was maths, my worst subject. I knew I wasn't going to pass before I walked in. I just didn't get numbers. Even now I use my fingers to add up. That night there was a leaving party in Hollywood's and I was more concerned about that and my outfit for it than I was about fractions and equations. There was a bouncer who worked on the door with a big scar across his face and I had taken a shine to him. I was looking forward to going and flirting with him. I had gone out that morning with some money Mum gave me and bought a new top and skirt from Miss Selfridge. My reluctance to get involved with boys seemed to desert me after my sixteenth birthday.

Mrs Francis was adjudicating the exam that afternoon and we filed in silently and sat at our seats waiting for the timer to begin.

'You can turn your papers over now,' she announced. I looked at the questions and scratched my head. I attempted to do as many as I could but in the back of my mind I could hear my mum's voice saying, 'Don't worry Gemma, you will be famous one day.' Halfway through the allotted time I put my pencil down, got up and said 'I'm finished'. Mrs Francis, who was looking down at her six toes, looked up at me quizzically. I smiled at her as I walked past. She didn't realise I had left half the questions blank (I got an ungraded mark for maths).

I walked out of school feeling liberated. It was all over. Then it hit me. What was I going to do? I felt that I was too grown-up to stay on and do sixth form and given the cost of the fees my parents didn't push me. I wanted to go to work. I had a Saturday job in Warehouse but that wasn't my chosen career. I wanted to be a performer, work in the media or be a reporter but I had no real plans. Except for Hollywood's, I had nowhere to go and I didn't care. I was going to be Britney Spears, I just had to find a way of getting there.

CHAPTER SEVEN

LOSING IT

That summer everything changed. I had grown up a lot at Raphael and although I eventually signed up to do a media studies course at Southend College, I felt I had outgrown school and education. I really wanted to work and earn my own money. While I waited to start college later in the year, I vowed to have as much fun as I possibly could.

And I couldn't do that if I was continually attending drama lessons. I had outgrown them. I wanted to go out with my friends more and I had started to discover boys.

Getting up and going to Sylvia Young on a Saturday was becoming a bind. It was cramping my style. I wanted to go to Romford and hang out with my friends instead. Mum was still keeping me busy all the time and I had begun it find it restrictive.

I resolved to tell her that I no longer wanted to go but I knew it would break her heart. My loyalties were torn. One Saturday, after returning from classes, I plucked up the courage. I didn't want to spend one more weekend at the drama school.

Mum was washing her nets in her bathroom. I went in and sat on her bed.

'Mum, I need to tell you something,' I began.

'What is it Gem?' she said.

'I think I've gone as far with Sylvia Young as I can, and I don't enjoy it any more. I want to leave.'

Mum had her back to me. She went quiet. Then I heard the sniffing. She came out of the bathroom and her eyes were red and glistening. She was crying. I was mortified. The last thing I wanted to do was upset her.

'Me and your dad have given you an opportunity to do this,' she said. 'I thought you enjoyed going.' It was not the right time to confess that I never truly enjoyed the school.

'I did, Mum,' I lied. 'But right now I don't think it is for me. I want to go to Romford with my mates and feel normal for a bit. I've been doing lessons at the weekend for ten years. It would be nice to have a break.'

Mum knew she couldn't make me go any longer, I wasn't a kid any more, and reluctantly she agreed that I should leave. Another chapter of my life was over.

I was going out more and enjoying the freedom leaving school had given me. It was a great summer. I was seeing more of Laura, my friend, and would stay over at her house at the weekend. Her dad, Kenny, was a bit of a character. He was a car dealer and he always wore black and rode a Harley-Davidson motorbike. His wife, Sadie, was a character too. One Saturday night they were having a barbecue and I was invited over to keep Laura company. Around 8.30 p.m. we started to get itchy feet and hatched a plan to get to the local pub without arousing suspicion. We'd tell Kenny we were going to the supermarket to buy some sweets but instead would head to the Unicorn in nearby Gidea Park because that's where all the boys were. We convinced Kenny that we wouldn't be long and he agreed on the condition that we were back by 10 p.m. I whacked on the Revlon ColourStay mascara and ushered Laura out the front door. She was nervous. She didn't like lying to her dad.

'Come on,' I urged, 'you only live once.'

The pub was heaving and there were loads of people we knew in there. There were boys everywhere and our eyes were popping out of our heads. I ordered us both an Archers and lemonade and we headed over to a group of older boys we knew and started chatting to them. We both forgot about the time and a couple of drinks later Laura looked at her watch and started to panic. It was past ten o'clock.

'Come on Gemma,' she implored, 'we have to go now. Dad will be mad.'

'Just relax,' I soothed. 'He won't mind if we are a little late. We'll tell him we met some friends at the supermarket.'

We stayed for what we thought was a short while longer but when I looked at the clock on the wall it said 11.10. Laura's face went white when she realised the time.

'Don't worry, I have a plan,' I told her. 'We'll wind our watches back and tell Kenny that they both stopped and that we met some friends and thought it was still 10 p.m.'

Laura raised an eyebrow.

'Honestly, it will work. Trust me,' I shrugged.

We left the pub and ran back to Laura's house. Just before turning in to her street we stopped, wound our watches back and caught our breath. We walked to the front door. Laura didn't have keys. As she rang the doorbell I whispered under my breath.

'Act cool, don't say a word, let me do the talking.'

Kenny answered with a face like thunder. His all-black outfit added to the general air of malevolence.

'What time do you call this?' he hissed. 'It's 11.30!'

It was as if the drama switch had been flipped on in my head. I called on all my acting skills and theatrically raised my hand and looked at my watch.

'What do you mean Kenny?' I gasped. 'My watch says 10 p.m. We met some friends and were chatting to them, my watch must have stopped.'

Laura looked at hers.

'Mine's stopped too,' she said unconvincingly.

Kenny shook his head.

'Do you think I was born yesterday? Get upstairs to bed.'

The barbecue was still in full swing but we were sent to Laura's room. The next morning Kenny was fine with us though. He had been young once and I think secretly he thought the escapade was funny.

In Essex, parties were a big thing. They still are. Essex people look for any excuse for a get-together and many use it as a way of showing off their big houses. The more extravagant they are, the better. Throughout my late teenage years, life was a constant round of parties and barbecues. I had developed a huge social circle and would get invited to more dos than my parents.

The summer after I left school, Laura's parents' friends were having a party. It was the husband's fortieth birthday and I was invited. At the time I had my eye on a boy called Greg. He was older, around nineteen. I told Laura that I fancied him when were in the local park one day and she mentioned that he would be at the party, so when I got the invite I had butterflies. He was so good-looking. I had seen him around in some of the pubs I went to and flirted with him. There was chemistry between us. I could tell that he fancied me. The day before the party I went to Romford Market to a stall there that sold Morgan dresses, which were slinky and sexy. I got myself a black clingy number and slipped into it on the night of the do with a plan to snare Greg hatching in my mind.

When it came to men I was a late developer. Most of my friends had already had several boyfriends and many had lost their virginity. I was private when it came to talking to boys and while a lot of my friends assumed I had already had sex because of my confidence, I was actually one of the last. Sixteen is late for an Essex girl!

I had a lovely tingling of nerves when I walked into the party in my tight black dress and saw Greg sitting on the sofa in the lounge chatting to a couple of other boys. He looked gorgeous. He was wearing a pale blue shirt and dark jeans. His hair was slicked with gel and he was clean-shaven. He had a smile that made me melt and when I walked in he looked up. Our eyes met and I smiled shyly.

I went into the kitchen to get myself a Malibu and pineapple to steady my nerves.

I grabbed Laura.

'He's here, he looks amaze,' I swooned.

'He likes you Gem, you can tell. When you walked into the kitchen his eyes followed you.'

'This is it Laura,' I giggled. 'I'm going to talk to him.'

I knocked back my drink, poured another and went over to chat to him. I was going to make him mine that night. He was going to get some Gemma candy!

I sidled up to him on the sofa.

'Hi Greg, I like your shirt,' I purred.

He smiled at me and we fell into easy conversation. I asked him whether he had a girlfriend and he said he didn't.

'I don't believe it. A good-looking boy like you must have girls throwing themselves at you,' I said.

'You're not so bad yourself,' he laughed.

There was electricity between us. Our thighs were touching and I could feel the heat of his body. He leaned in to me.

'Shall we go somewhere a bit quieter?' he asked.

My stomach was turning cartwheels.

'OK,' I stuttered.

Quietly we sneaked up the stairs and found an empty bedroom. Greg pulled me down next to him on the bed. We didn't need to talk. Our lips met and the thrill of excitement that shot through me was intense.

I felt ready for him and awkwardly we had sex. There was nothing seedy about it. It wasn't passionate, I was nervous and it felt nice but weird. I wouldn't say I enjoyed it. It didn't last long and afterwards we awkwardly rearranged our clothes and rejoined the party. I had gone into the room a girl and when I came out I was a woman. I felt proud that I had done it. I had no regrets at all.

I never told Greg that he was my first. We saw each other a couple of times after because we hung around with the same group but our relationship never went anywhere. I wasn't bothered. I didn't feel used at all; basically we had used each other to get what we wanted.

Despite my fumble with Greg, I still had not had a proper long-term boyfriend. I'd had a few dates but I was kept so busy for most of my teenage years with drama and singing that I never had time. But I was growing up and becoming more aware of my sexuality and more curious about the opposite sex.

I wasn't shy, I liked boys and I liked hanging out with them. At the all-girls' school I had led a sheltered life but attending mixed school for that last year of my education had brought me into contact with plenty of boys. At Raphael I was in a class with a boy called Matthew. I became very friendly with him. He was a lovely guy, not my type but a lot of fun to be around and we moved in the same social circles so would often meet up as a group. Matthew had an older brother, John. Our paths had crossed on several occasions but I'd never spent much time with him. He was very good-looking though and I fancied him.

On Matthew's seventeenth birthday a large group of us celebrated at Ritzy (I was now going to the proper club nights, not the underage ones) and John was there with a few of his friends. Something about him made him stand out from the crowd. He was always smart. He wore Gant clothes, pastel shirts, nice jeans and loafers. He carried off that preppie look naturally. He looked like he had money and class. His blond hair was swept back and he was tall and lithe. He looked like a male version of me at the time as I was blonde, tall and slim too.

That night I spent time talking to him and he told me about himself. He was studying to become a million and one things. He wanted to become an airline pilot. He had just finished university and he was looking for work. He had a motorbike, a red Mazda MX2 with black leather seats, and he had a charming personality.

It wasn't an immediate electric attraction but I warmed to him and we got on extremely well. At the end of the night he gave me a kiss goodnight and asked if we could perhaps go out some time. I agreed enthusiastically and over the next few weeks we fell into an easy friendship. We'd meet up for drinks or coffee and chat about our lives. He was very easy to be around.

As our relationship developed we both started to sense that we were becoming more than just friends. Each time we said goodbye there was an awkward moment when we went to kiss each other on the cheek and both hesitated. I felt the urge to go for the lips and so did John.

One day John took matters into his hands.

'I really like you Gemma,' he said, holding my gaze. 'Would you like to be my girlfriend?' It was quaint and lovely and he was going for broke. If I said no it would compromise our friendship. But my heart was dancing.

'Yeah, all right then,' I smiled. And that was it. The deal had been done and John became my first proper boyfriend. I was seventeen.

CHAPTER EIGHT

A TASTE OF ESSEX

Me, aged 12 months.
How cute was I?

Bath time on a camping
holiday in the south of France.

Me and my brother
Russell ready to party.

Come rain or shine, I was always up for dressing up.

Looking as good as gold (aged 15) in my school uniform.

Proof that fairies do live at the bottom of the garden.

Hula time! On holiday at Potters holiday camp.

Showing off again!

The Collins Family.
A spooky snap of me,
Mum and Russell at
Center Parcs.

Backstage at one of
our shows, daaahling.

Remember darling....
I'm your best friend

A pretty girl in
a pretty dress.

Blingtastic! Another night, another show.

Prancing around in my undies. I can't believe how slim I was back then!

Nuns on the run.
Me and my co-star in
The Sound of Music.

All aboard! Fun in the
sun on a boat in Turkey.

My amazing dad
and me having a
paddle in Mallorca.

Bikini shot. Yes,
that gorgeous
girl really is me!

Me and my beautiful nephews Hayden and Kane.

Me and Mum. I love her with all my heart.

ohn's parents were minted (that's Essex for rich) and dating John was my first introduction to proper Essex money. I'd been around rich kids and their parents before. I met plenty of them at private school. But I had never gone out with one.

Growing up in Essex had filled me with aspiration. I wanted the big house and the flash car. Mum instilled in me the belief that you should always go for quality. When I was a little girl I remember watching *GMTV* and seeing the news that Princess Di had been on holiday to a posh resort called Sandy Lane in Barbados. I turned to Mum and said, 'I'm going to go there one day.' And years later I did, when Cassie got married there. The message is that something in me aspired to that lifestyle.

I knew Essex was a glam place. I used to go to restaurants with my mum and dad and see how the older women dressed. Mum was always dolled up and that Essex glamour has always been in my blood. From a young age I dreamed of the high life because it was always on my doorstep. As I got older I knew I had two routes to get where I wanted to go; I could meet a rich man who would look after me (the dream of lots of Essex girls) or I would have to work hard and get there myself.

I've always worked. After I left school I took a job waitressing at the local pub, the Orange Tree. I didn't tell Mum and Dad at first because I knew they wouldn't be happy. They wanted me to have a nice part-time job in a clothes shop, which I still had, in Warehouse, not in a pub where there was the heady cocktail of boys and booze. Initially when I started to go out every Friday night I told them I was with John. It was a half-truth because John drank in the pub and would usually be in there when I was working. My uniform was a pair of sparkly black Topshop trousers and a black top. I took the job because I genuinely liked chatting to people. I was terrible at waitressing though. I used to drop the knives and forks in the pints. It was a nightmare. I did eventually confess to Mum what I was doing and she was mortified. But I was no longer a little girl and there wasn't much she could do about it.

Life with John was full of excitement. His family owned care homes. They had a speedboat and on Saturdays we went out on it. Their house was amazing. It was massive with big electric iron gates that opened on to a sweeping driveway. As huge as it was, it had a warm feel to it. It also had its own riding stables and a pool.

John's mum, Marge, was a real character; a stunning woman. She was always curling her hair. I loved her from the minute I met her.

The family had a holiday home in Spain, an apartment with a pool. Marge spent a lot of time there. It seemed she was there more than she was in the UK. When I first started dating John I didn't meet her for several weeks because she was in Spain. She knew all about me though because her husband had told her his son was seeing a girl. I don't think I ever saw Marge in the same outfit twice.

When I did meet her, we got on like a house on fire and she told me she was going back to Spain in a couple of weeks and asked if I would I like to go with her. I was on an extended summer holiday because my college course didn't start until later in the year, so off I went with her for a month. It was a fantastic time; John had started work for a financial firm and he took holiday and came with us, then flew back when he needed to get back to work.

The apartment was on a complex a short walk from the beach. It had a pool and I spent my days sunbathing, alternating between the pool and the beach. In the evenings we would go into town for dinner and few sangrias. John and I were never into clubbing, we were always out doing activities like boating or family parties. I am really quite a homely girl.

After that first long holiday I used to pop backwards and forwards to Spain on a regular basis. John, who was two years older than I was, had another brother called Michael who had a girl-friend called Samantha. Marge, Samantha and I used to trot off to Spain every few months. I could afford it by taking on extra shifts at work. After the first trip to Spain I left my job at Warehouse and got one in Benetton, which was better paid. I was young and 250 pesetas seemed to last a lifetime. Dad was very generous too. He always used to give me my holiday spending money. Marge looked after us when we were there. She only had sons so we were like the daughters she never had. The whole family was very good to me and very generous. On my eighteenth birthday they bought me a gold Gucci watch with a mother-of-pearl face and at Christmas Marge bought me Tiffany jewellery.

I would class John as my first love. We had a lovely relationship. He was fun to be around and he was romantic. We were still only young though and I had a wandering eye. I never touched but I did like to look. And on one of those holidays in Spain my eyes fell on Carlos. It was like a scene from a movie. We were in his bar and while someone was singing 'Hero' on the karaoke, I watched as he walked out from behind the bar flicking back his dark mane of hair. His white shirt, open to his chest, strained to contain a pair of impressive pecs.

'Corrr!' I purred under my breath.

Carlos was a typical Spanish Romeo. All the girls in Carlos's bar were there because of him. The karaoke, live Sky Sports and cheap cocktails were just trappings. The main event was Carlos.

I felt an instant animal attraction. Carlos became the highlight of my holidays and most nights when I was in Spain and not with John would end up with a trip to his bar. I was mesmerised by him.

After that long summer the time came to start at college. I still wasn't sure what I wanted to do. I harboured dreams of fame and fortune but didn't know how I was going to make those dreams come true. So on a dreary day in October I set out on the bus to start a media studies course at Southend College; or South Essex College of Further and Higher Education as it is now called. I didn't know what media studies were but hoped the course would give me some qualifications to be a journalist or a celebrity.

It was a culture shock going from a small private school to a large anonymous campus. The college was one of the largest in the east of England and it seemed like there were thousands of students. As soon as I arrived I had reservations. The people there were nice and I made friends easily but I didn't feel right there.

'This isn't for me,' I thought to myself. The best discovery I made on that first day was the hot chocolate in the college canteen.

I stuck it out for a few weeks but I just didn't get media studies. It was a lot of theory and was all about different types of media and mass communication. I thought it would be more practical but instead it was about social science and communication theory. It wasn't going to be much use to me when I went to castings for acting jobs! It bored the hell out of me and after three weeks my attendance started to slip. I would tell Mum and Dad that there were no lectures and stay at home or go out with friends. Eventually the college called home and told my dad that I hadn't been going. I think he was exasperated more than he was angry. He didn't know what to do with me and I didn't know what to do with myself.

'I don't like it there Dad,' I explained. 'The course isn't relevant to what I want to do.'

'What do you want to do?' he asked.

'I'm not sure,' I shrugged.

'There's no point you going if you are not going to get anything out of it, you might as well leave but you really need to think about your future Gemma, you can't just drift through life,' he conceded.

I needed some headspace. I needed to get away and clear my mind and work out what I was going to do. I hatched a plan and called Vicky.

'Do you fancy going to Spain, just us, no boys?' I asked.

That was my plan. To go on holiday where I could think about my future. John was working so he was happy. We used the apartment and took Vicky's younger sister Lisa. It was my first girls-only holiday and we had a blast. We weren't on the lookout for boys,

I was in a relationship with John and wasn't that sort of girl. We chilled and sunbathed in the days and at nights would go for a dance and a drink. The highlight of the whole week was going down to Carlos's.

On the last night I wanted to put on a show to try and catch his eye and I put my name down for the karaoke. When it was my turn the girls cheered as I took to the stage.

The opening bars of Madonna's 'Crazy For You' crackled over the tinny sound system.

I looked at Carlos and started singing.

Carlos continued pouring drinks behind the bar, oblivious to my serenade.

'I'm crazy for you … touch me once …' I belted out.

My efforts went unnoticed and although we had some fun banter with Carlos, my interest in him remained an innocent infatuation. He was much older than I was and I suspect that if he had ever reciprocated my obvious flirting I would have run a mile. Not copping off with Carlos didn't tarnish the holiday however. It was a wonderful, fun, carefree week and gave me the taste for holidays in later life.

Back at home I was still no nearer knowing what I wanted to do with the rest of my life and was back to working in Benetton, which I loved, but I always knew it was not what I was going to do full time. Marge offered a solution.

'Are you going to get a job then Gemma?' she asked.

'I suppose so,' I replied. 'But I don't know what I want to do.'

'Well, why don't you work in one of our care homes for the time being until you decide what you want to do,' she said. 'And

I'll have a chat with a few of my friends and see if we can get you something more permanent.'

I accepted gratefully and two days later I started working in a home in Essex looking after people suffering from mental illness. I would help them get dressed, help them eat, assist them on days out and look after their general well-being.

It was a million miles away from being famous but I enjoyed it and I became very attached to the patients there. The job only lasted a couple of weeks however – Marge had spoken to one of her friends who owned a recruitment agency in London and mentioned that she knew me and that I was looking for a job. The woman's name was Sarah and Marge told me to give her a call, which I did. We arranged to meet. I liked the idea of working in London, I'd spent so much time there with Mum it wasn't daunting. When I met Sarah I was enthusiastic about the prospect and it must have showed as she offered me a job there and then.

I started the following week. I wore a dark power suit so I would look the part. The job was selling the recruitment agency's services to other businesses. It was basically telesales but we were selling people rather than products. I would call up a company and give them the spiel about what we could offer and the quality of candidates we had on our books. It came very naturally to me and from the beginning I enjoyed it. I had always been a good talker, able to connect with people and think on my feet, qualities which meant that I excelled. I had found something I was good at and that in turn filled me with the confidence that the job demanded.

Times were good. I was working in London and I was getting paid for it. I loved being in the buzz of the big city and getting dressed up to go to work each day. I also had a rich boyfriend who I adored and I could flit to Spain whenever I fancied.

Life with John settled into a comfortable routine. We enjoyed each other's company and we had plenty of laughs. My world was expanding and that, in part, was due to John; he was older and more experienced and his wealthy background meant that he had seen a bit of the world. When I was seventeen I even tried drugs for the first time. I didn't intend to. I have always been against drugs; I think they are a sign of weakness. I took them by accident.

It was late August when me, John and some mates went to stay with some friends for the weekend. I was looking forward to getting into my bikini and having a sunbathe in the garden in the glorious sunshine. But I was famished and first I needed to eat. I went to the kitchen in search of something to eat. They had a lovely big kitchen with a central island and a double range cooker. The smell when I walked in was divine. Someone had been baking. I spied the source of the smell; a plate of rock cakes on the side by the kettle. I grabbed one to have with the cup of tea I was making.

The cake was dry and it had a strange flavour to it. There were flecks of some sort of green herb in it. I tried to work out if it was oregano or perhaps sage. It was strange combination in a rock cake but I was too hungry to care. I grabbed another, wolfed it down and went upstairs to change into my bikini.

It was while I was in the bathroom washing off my eye make-up that I started to feel very peculiar. My arms and legs began to feel very heavy and my vision started to blur. I started to sweat and I could feel my heart racing. I couldn't work out what was happening to me and I started to panic. This, in turn, increased my heart rate more. I was panting and my body felt too heavy to bear. I crumpled on the floor as the room started to swim in front of my eyes.

I managed to crawl to the bed and lay on top of it, pale and out of breath. John came into the room.

'Oh my God, what's wrong?' He took one look at me and knew I wasn't well. 'You look terrible.'

'I feel terrible,' I croaked. 'I think I need to be sick. The room is spinning.'

'Have you been drinking?' John asked.

'No, I just came in, had a cup of tea and a cake and now I feel sick,' I explained.

John hesitated for a minute.

'Er … what cake did you eat Gemma?' he asked nervously.

'The ones in the kitchen,' I replied.

'How many did you have?' He looked worried.

'Only two, they tasted funny, I didn't want any more than that.' My speech was slurred and my eyes were feeling heavy. I suddenly felt very drowsy.

'Shit!' exclaimed John. 'Those are hash cakes Gem, one of the lads brought them.'

I had never taken drugs before. I didn't know what to expect. I was terrified.

'Oh God, John,' I started to cry. 'Am I going to die, have I overdosed? Please call an ambulance.'

'Listen, just relax Gem and stay calm. It'll be fine, you can't OD on hash cakes, you'll feel better in a while,' he reassured me. 'I'll stay here with you until you feel better.'

And that's how I had my first and last experience with drugs, by accident thanks to my weakness for cake. Ironically, food became a sort of drug for me later in life, which I relied on in times of trouble. That night John lay with me while I drifted in and out of sleep. I can't say I enjoyed the experience. I just felt sick and then drowsy. I stayed in bed all evening and slept it off. The next day I felt terrible and it took a couple of days to shake off the feeling.

We had a lot of friends and John knew some colourful characters. His best friend was a girl called Leah. They had grown up together and Leah was an old friend of his family. She was a lovely girl, very beautiful and she had lovely parents: Myra and Stan. Myra looked like a model and Stan used to be in a pop band. They were big in the sixties and hailed from Dagenham. A few years after they formed they were auditioned by one of the major labels and were in competition with another band the label was interested in signing. The band won and went on to have a long career. The band they beat was the Beatles! Through dating John I was introduced to Leah, her family and her partner, a larger-than-life bloke called Ben. He was nineteen and reminded me of Del Boy. He was extremely lovely-looking in my eyes. I warmed to him as soon as I met him. I couldn't help myself. He had dark curly hair that he used to gel. He looked Jewish or Mediterranean. The first time I met Ben was at his wedding to Leah. I was invited as John's plus one. John told me that it would be a very plush do. Ben had his own electrician business and loved to give it large but often didn't have £10 to his name. His parents were well off however and Leah's had plenty of money. The wedding was in a beautiful country hotel and I wore a long, white, beaded and sequinned dress. It was massively over the top and I didn't even realise that by wearing white I was in danger of upstaging the bride. I chose it because I was told we were going to a really fancy do.

I had heard a lot about Leah and I was nervous about meeting her but equally excited about going to an Essex society wedding. It was a lovely day and lived up to the expectations. Leah and Ben looked very happy together and after that day we started seeing them regularly. A year later they had a son.

Ben had the swagger that I found attractive and I couldn't help getting on with him, even if he could be coarse. I loved John but I always had a thing for Ben. He was flash and brash. We would go out as a foursome and he would order bottles of Bollinger and make a scene about it. He could be really embarrassing on occasion but he was good fun. Leah was the complete opposite, she was quiet. People assumed John and Leah were together and that Ben and I were partners. I got to know his parents, Sandra and Harry, and got on famously with them. They had regular parties, which John and I was always invited to. Often I would find myself looking at Ben and wishing that John was a bit more like him.

Ben lived for the day. He was impulsive. When he had money he would spend it and when he didn't have money he would spend someone else's. One night he called us up.

'Right you two, we're going to the Hilton on Park Lane for a drink in Windows on the World. Be ready at seven. I've laid on the transport,' he ordered.

The Park Lane Hilton is a top London hotel. With twenty-eight floors it towers over Hyde Park. Windows on the World is a posh bar on the top floor, fitted with floor to ceiling windows that give customers an amazing view out over the city. Ben had booked a table at a charity event that was being held there. It was a black-tie event so I wore a ballgown and John got dressed up in his black tuxedo.

Just after seven there was a knock on the door.

'Your chariot awaits,' beamed Ben, ushering us out of John's front door and on to the driveway. Gleaming on the asphalt was a blue vintage Bentley. It was a proper old-fashioned car.

'What are we going in that old thing for?' I exclaimed. It was the Essex girl in me talking. I didn't realise or appreciate that it was a rare classic car. I wanted a stretch limo. I wanted glitz and glamour. John and Ben exchanged a look and both raised their eyebrows.

The night was a blast, made even more entertaining by Ben who went overboard at the charity auction and bid for most of the lots.

Around the same time I was enjoying the company of Ben and his larger-than-life antics I also met another man who became an important figure in my life: Robert.

I met him in Faces nightclub, my favourite nightclub in Essex until the Sugar Hut stole its crown. It was Christmas and I was nineteen years old and I'd been invited there by a friend of mine, Carly. She was having a party there. There was group of us meeting for a meal and I went along on my own. John was busy.

Although I didn't know many of the people who were going, I rarely turned down a chance to go to Faces. It was the place to be. It had only been opened a few years and it was the most talked-about club outside of the West End. It had a VIP guest list from the world of TV, fashion and sport. It had six bars, two rooms of music and VIP tables, and it was where footballers went. It was a favourite haunt of players from Tottenham and West Ham. Many of them lived in and around the area. Jamie Redknapp and Teddy Sheringham were regulars. Teddy's jacket once got tangled up in the straps of my Dior handbag there. You literally could rub shoulders with Premiership footballers and many girls went just to try and snare themselves a rich player. Although it was supposed to be an exclusive members-only club, it was easy to get in if you were glamorous enough and the doormen would let in girls they fancied so the trick was to flirt with them. If you were an Essex girl and you got into Faces it was like having a golden ticket. It was very much the scene to be in. You would dress up the same as you would if you were going in to the West End. Blokes would dress to impress; £400 designer chinos and a blazer were not out of the ordinary. Everyone made a real effort. On the night I met Robert I wore a gold halter-neck dress from Warehouse with diamantes sewn around the hem and neckline.

Robert had a twinkle in his eye. I walked into the club and found Carly and her party and he was sitting at the table they were on talking to another man I didn't know. He looked up and smiled at me, then excused himself from the conversation he was having and introduced himself.

'Hi, I'm Robert,' he said, holding out his hand. I shook and told him my name. We made easy small talk about the club and who we did and didn't know at the table.

Robert wasn't what I would normally go for and there was no physical attraction but he did make me laugh. He was comfortable and friendly. I warmed to him immediately.

For the rest of the night Robert and me stuck to each other's side like glue. He was generous and bought drinks for everyone. It

was clear he wasn't short of a few quid. He told me he was a financial trader in the City, he worked for one of the big stockbroking
companies there. It was a very stressful job, he explained, but the
rewards were huge. He was a few years older than I was and lived
with his parents but was thinking of moving out and buying a flat
of his own.

The night went quickly and we had a lot of fun. It was sweet
the way Robert looked after me because he knew I was on my own.
At around one in the morning I had started to tire and was ready
to leave. I told him I was going to get a cab home.

'Let me take you,' he said. 'I've had enough and I need to
be up for work in the morning anyway. A beautiful girl like you
shouldn't be travelling home alone.'

I cringed a little and blushed.

'Sure, why not?' I said.

We said goodbye to the others and jumped in a taxi outside the
club. When the cab reached my house I turned to say goodbye and
give him a peck on the cheek.

'Er,' he hesitated, 'can I come in for a coffee?' He stuttered and
looked awkward when he asked.

I was taken aback. I genuinely didn't understand why he was
asking. Was he thirsty? I was still naive when it came to men and
their ways and I genuinely though Robert wanted a drink. I didn't
realise that 'coming in for coffee' means something more than a
cup of Nescafé.

'Sure,' I said, 'we've only got Nescafé though, I think it's
Gold Blend.'

Robert laughed.

'You are funny Gemma,' he said.

We got out of the cab and Robert paid.

'How will you get back?' I asked.

'I'll order another cab a bit later,' he said.

I started to wonder how long he thought he would be staying. I was knackered so when we got indoors I put the kettle on, flicked on the TV for Robert and went upstairs to put my dressing gown and pyjamas on. I thought it would give him the hint that I was ready for bed and that he shouldn't overstay his welcome. When I came back down Robert had made himself comfortable. He'd kicked off his shoes and had undone a button on his shirt. He was sprawled on the couch (the old second-hand one had been replaced by a comfy fabric John Lewis one a few years previously and, by that time, Mum and Dad had even splashed out on a new kitchen). He was watching some late-night rubbish on the TV.

I made Robert his coffee and we chatted. Every now and then I would punctuate our talk with a yawn, just to make sure he realised he wasn't going to be there for hours. I didn't mind but I didn't want to wake Mum and Dad up who were asleep upstairs.

'You finished that drink yet Robert?' I asked after about half an hour. I reinforced the question with another yawn and an exaggerated stretch. Finally the penny dropped.

'Of course,' he said. 'You must be knackered, I'll call a cab.'

We waited ten minutes for the cab to arrive and when we heard it pull up outside Robert got his shoes on and stood.

'It's been really good meeting you Gemma,' he said. 'We should do it again.'

'Yeah,' I nodded. 'It was a good night.'

'What's your number then?' asked Robert casually. 'I'll give you a call and we'll sort something out in the next few weeks.'

We exchanged numbers innocently and I pecked him on the cheek and told him to give me a call.

The next morning he texted me and thanked me for the coffee.

'I met a bloke called Robert last night,' I told John later that day. It turned out John knew him.

'He came back for coffee,' I said.

A look crossed John's face.

'Coffee?' he asked accusingly.

'Yeah, I gave him a cup of Nescafé. I thought it was weird.'

'He fancies you,' said John.

I laughed. The idea sounded ludicrous. Robert just wasn't my type.

But over the following weeks he called me regularly. He knew I was with John and as far as I was concerned I had gained a new friend. He was kind and loyal and he was always interested in what I was doing. One afternoon soon after we met he called me out of the blue.

'What are you up to later?' he said. 'I've got tickets to a gig in town, do you want to come?'

Robert used to get a lot of tickets to events through his work and more often than not he'd ask me to go with him. He was single and I wasn't stupid, I realised that he liked having me around because I was female company, but he never made a pass at me and our relationship never crossed the line between friends and romance. There just wasn't that spark there as far as I was concerned. John would sometimes comment, but because Robert wasn't the best-looking bloke in the world John didn't feel Robert's presence in my social circle was a threat.

As I approached the two-year anniversary with John, I began to become aware that things were changing between us. The initial excitement I had about being with him had faded and our relationship felt tired. We still got on but I wanted to spread my wings and so did John. We never really argued but I could feel things fading between us. It made me sad but also I had started to question whether it was time to move on. I had turned twenty and I felt different about life. I was growing up.

John in turn had begun to appear distracted. He was spending more time with his friends and I began to wonder if we were just together out of habit rather than because we wanted to be with each other.

While I was friends with Robert and would go out with him on occasion, John had formed a friendship with a girl who he worked with. I trusted John but I had a gut instinct about her that I couldn't shake. I had seen some over familiar texts on his phone from her and whenever I called his office she answered and, although she was polite, there was something in her tone that made alarm bells ring in my head.

I asked John about her on several occasions. In the same way he suspected Robert fancied me, I suspected she fancied him. John would laugh off my accusations and I would feel guilty for broaching the subject.

'Don't be silly Gemma,' he would tut, 'she's just a girl I work with.'

One Sunday I was having dinner at John's with him and his mum and we were chatting about the week.

John was explaining that he'd been lazing around that morning and hadn't been up to much.

'You fixed that girl's car though this morning didn't you John?' Marge said.

John's face reddened immediately.

'Er, oh yeah,' he stuttered.

'What girl?' I asked.

'That girl from his work,' Marge said. 'She came up here.'

I looked at John and he looked crestfallen. There was guilt written all over his face. I could tell from the way he looked that he'd wanted to cover up the fact the he'd seen her that morning. The only conclusion I could draw was that he didn't want me to know because he was trying to hide something. Jealousy and hurt bubbled up inside me. All this time he'd made me feel bad for questioning him about his relationship with her and now he'd been caught red-handed.

I couldn't control what I did next. I picked up a piece of broccoli from my plate, still dripping with gravy, and I flung it straight at his face. He flinched as it hit him on the cheek and left green and brown splatters on his white shirt.

I got up from the table and stormed off upstairs, leaving Marge open-mouthed. John ran after me.

'What did you do that for?' he accused.

'You know exactly why. What's going on between you and her?' I demanded. 'Why didn't you tell me she came here earlier? You tried to hide it.'

'I didn't tell you because I know you think there's something going on and I knew you'd overreact,' he said, wiping gravy from his face. 'She's a friend from work and I agreed to help her fix her car, that's all there is to it.'

I wasn't convinced but I had no way of knowing whether he was telling the truth or not. We had been a couple for two years and the least he deserved was the benefit of the doubt. I calmed down and went back to finish lunch, but for the rest of the day the atmosphere between us was strained and I was relieved to leave early in the evening.

I hoped that we were just going through a bad patch in our relationship and that things would sort themselves out but although John and I limped on for another couple of weeks, I knew that something had broken between us and in my heart of hearts I didn't believe it could be fixed. I no longer trusted him.

We didn't see very much of each other for the two weeks following our spat over lunch. I was still working in recruitment in London and was putting in long hours. I had gone from strength to strength professionally. I always knew that recruitment wasn't my future. I never looked at it as a long-term career but I was still enjoying what I did and the company I worked for was doing very well. I was benefitting from some very generous bonuses and in some months would be able to earn up to £3000. But I enjoyed spending it. A few years before, I had signed up for a credit card and it had become my best friend. I relied on it and enjoyed the freedom it allowed me to go on guilt-free spending splurges. I figured with the money I was earning and the hours I was working, I deserved to treat myself. I was building up an impressive collection of shoes and handbags. The bills had begun to sting a little each month and so I was working harder to meet the payments.

I was working later and when the weekends came I would often just want to kick back and relax. So, a fortnight after our argument when we were due to attend the wedding of one of John's cousins, I wasn't feeling up to going.

I called John and told him apologetically. He sounded annoyed.

'We've been planning this for months,' he said. I felt bad because I really liked his cousin but my heart just wasn't in it. I saw John later that day and we had a heart-to-heart chat.

'This isn't working Gemma,' he said. 'I think we need to call it a day.'

Even though I knew things were not great between us I couldn't imagine not having John in my life.

Tears stung my eyes. I didn't want it to end but I knew in my heart that it was over.

'We'll still be best of friends,' he told me. 'I think the world of you Gemma, you know I do.'

I nodded sadly and that was it. John dumped me. I knew it was right to part but that didn't stop it hurting. It was a very sad time because I did love him. We had been together all that time and we had some very happy memories. For a few days I was at a loss. I didn't know what to do with myself and my heart was heavy. I knew my world wasn't over. I realised I was young and I had plenty of living to do but I was sad that John wasn't part of my life anymore.

Mum, as ever, had some sound words of advice.

'I wish it had worked out,' I told her.

'You very rarely end up with your first love,' she replied. 'It's never nice breaking up with someone but you are still young Gemma. Cry, get over it and move on. Be careful what you wish for when you are young. You have a whole life to live before you need to worry about things like love.'

And that's what I did. I was sad for a few weeks and then I got on with life.

John and I didn't remain the good friends I thought we would. We didn't see each other for a while after we parted and soon after we did I heard news that made our break-up easier to handle. John had started seeing the girl from his work. I knew my instincts had been correct. He might not have been seeing her when we were together but I was sure he had feelings for her then and was looking for a way out of our relationship.

After the split Robert was there to offer his support. He was a good friend and a shoulder to cry on. He would call me every day to make sure I was OK and he took me out for meals to keep me busy. I was happy to have someone in my life I could rely on.

CHAPTER NINE

FINDING MR (ALMOST) RIGHT

Robert was more than just emotional support for me. He was interested in helping me in my career too. He knew I enjoyed the job I was doing and was keen to help me progress. He was doing well as a trader and earning a healthy wage and his generosity knew no bounds. Robert had faith in my abilities and he made me an offer that took me by surprise.

One night, soon after I'd broken up with John, he took me for an Italian meal in Upminster, an expensive suburb near east London.

The conversation turned to the future.

'So Gemma,' said Robert, shifting forward in his seat after a large plate of seafood linguini, 'what are your plans?'

'I was going to have the tiramisu,' I teased.

'You know what I'm talking about,' he laughed. 'What are your plans for the future?'

I was still just twenty and thought at the time it was quite a serious question to be asking.

'I'm not sure to be honest,' I answered.

'I like my job but it's not what I want to do for the rest of my life. I want to find a rich bloke to look after me,' I laughed.

Robert had a faraway look in his eye.

'What if I offered to help you out?' he asked. He looked serious.

'What do you mean?'

He tapped a spoon casually on the table.

'Well, I'm doing well at work. I have some money put aside and I'm looking to invest in a business,' he said.

I wondered what he was saying.

'Go on ...' I said.

'Well, you're good at what you do. You make that company you work for good money. You have contacts in the industry. How would you fancy running your own recruitment agency?'

'I'm not sure Robert,' I said. 'It's a big step from working in an agency to running one.'

'I didn't mean right away,' said Robert. 'Why don't you carry on doing what you're doing and after a while, if it's still for you, I'll fund you and help you set up your own agency.'

It was a big offer. I didn't realise at the time but it was Robert's way of giving me a commitment for the future.

I was taken aback that he had such faith in me.

'That's a very generous offer Robert,' I said. I reached over the table and squeezed his hand. 'I'll definitely give it serious thought.'

In the back of mind however, I could hear my mum. 'You're going to be famous one day Gemma'. I still had dreams of another life; one where I wasn't confined to an office and where fame and fortune beckoned.

After the meal Robert asked if I wanted to go back to his house and meet his parents. They lived just across the road from the restaurant. He was moving out and had just exchanged contracts on a modern apartment and was looking forward to having the freedom of his own place. Robert paid the bill and walked me across to his house. His mum and dad were watching TV in the lounge.

'Hello love, we've heard a lot about you,' beamed his mum when he introduced me. I gave her a hug and we chatted about my parents and my job and the meal we'd just eaten.

Robert's parents were lovely. They were salt of the earth people and very proud of their son. I warmed to them and got to know them well over the following weeks as Robert prepared to move. He had asked me to help him with the move and on the day he completed contracts I drove up to his parents' house in the Silver VW Polo my dad had bought me when I passed my test several months earlier.

'We're not going to get much in here Robert,' I laughed. 'Is there a van coming?'

'No,' he shrugged, 'it's just us.'

I wondered why, of all the friends he had, he only chose me to help him move.

'I'm not going to be much use with the heavy stuff,' I apologised.

'That's OK, there isn't any. All the furniture is new, it's being delivered.'

It was his first house and he was starting from scratch. We spent the day flitting between Robert's parents' house and his new flat, ferrying boxes of boy's stuff between the two properties. There were books, CDs, DVDs, kitchenware, clothes and towels.

It was hard work, but fun. It was good to see Robert so obviously houseproud. He kept telling me how glad he was to having a woman helping him and would ask my advice on where to put things. Later in the day some of the furniture started to arrive. Robert busied himself putting together the bed when it was delivered and it was followed by a sofa and dining-room table and chairs. The flat slowly took shape.

'It's a lovely place,' I told him when we stopped for lunch.

'Yes it is,' he mused. 'But it's not a long-term thing. Eventually I want a house somewhere in the country.'

'What's your dream house?' I asked absently.

'A barn conversion,' he replied.

I gasped. 'No way. That's my ideal home too,' I told him.

'One day you'll live in one,' he said smiling.

It was exhausting but finally, in the early evening, the flat was looking like a cosy home. I thought a lot of Robert and I stayed helping out into the night because I wanted to be there for him the way he had been there for me after I broke up with John. But by 9 p.m. I was shattered and while Robert was in the living room fiddling with the TV I went for a lie-down on his bed.

I was drifting to sleep when I heard his footsteps in the hallway outside.

He pushed the door ajar and peeked round the corner. I lay still and didn't answer.

'You OK Gem?' he asked. I continued to be still and Robert started to worry.

'Gemma?' I could hear concern in his voice. I started to giggle.

'I thought you'd passed out with all the hard work,' he laughed.

'I needed a lie-down. I'm knackered,' I replied. 'I don't think I can do much more.'

He came into the room and sat on the bed next to me.

'It's been a long day but I really appreciate what you've done for me today,' he said. 'I couldn't have done it without you.'

He leaned over and put his arms around me. It was more than a cuddle between friends. I could feel the warmth of his body through his shirt and his breath on my shoulder. He rubbed my back.

'Thank you,' he whispered.

Through that cuddle I had the realisation that Robert perhaps wanted more than friendship from me. Had I been that naive? Had it been obvious all along? If I was honest with myself I probably had. It was obvious right from the time he sheepishly invited himself in for coffee.

I pulled away gently and smiled at him.

'That's what friends are for,' I said, forcing myself to be matter-of-fact. There were questions racing through my head. I was facing a dilemma. I thought a great deal of Robert. He was a lovely person. He was funny, he was kind and he was considerate. He was well-off and stable. In many respects he was a perfect man. But although I thought the world of him, there wasn't that spark. I didn't look at Robert and think 'Corrr!'

If you'd have asked me then what my ideal fella would be like, he would have been the same as he is today; a combination of my dad and Tony Soprano. I have always wanted a dependable man to look after me; someone who can make things right when they go wrong, someone reliable and strong. Someone who can make me feel secure. Robert had these qualities. But basically, I have also always looked for someone with a darker side. I like men who are edgy, I like gangsters and characters. It's all about the geezers. Robert was lovely, but he wasn't dodgy. And so, that night at his flat, I felt confused. The last thing I wanted to do was upset him. I valued our friendship very highly, Robert did too, which is why, I suspect, he didn't make a more obvious move on me. I needed time to think.

A few days later Robert took me out for a meal and drinks to say thank you and the awkward cuddle was not mentioned again.

We laughed and joked as normal and at the end of the night Robert told me that he had booked a holiday to Tenerife.

'I'm going in a few weeks,' he explained. He had booked an apartment in a complex with his brother Steve.

'Good for you,' I said. 'What I wouldn't give for a holiday.'

'Come with us,' he offered immediately.

I didn't know what to say.

'I'd love to,' I said. 'But I can't afford it.'

He persisted.

'Look Gemma, you did me a huge favour helping me move. You saved me loads of money on removal men. The least I can do is sort you out a holiday.'

'I couldn't …' I started. But Robert was having none of it. He was on a roll.

'It makes sense Gemma. I've already got a booking at the complex. I'll book another apartment. I'll sort out the flights. All you will need is some spending money.'

It was an attractive offer.

'Go on,' he pushed. 'It'll be a laugh.'

'Can I bring a couple of mates?' I asked. 'It'll be more of a laugh if there are more of us.'

'It's a deal,' he laughed.

Two weeks later me, two friends, Robert and Steve got a plane from Stansted Airport and headed off to Tenerife Town for some fun in the sun.

We had two apartments in a lovely complex right by the beach and bars at Playa de las Americas and from the first day we had fun. We messed around in the pool and on the beach. I was a slim size ten and enjoyed the opportunity to wear a bikini. Robert didn't have the best beach body but he didn't care and wasn't body-conscious. He enjoyed the opportunity to give everyone a good time and was more than generous when it came to buying drinks and food. In the evenings we'd hit the bars and the drink flowed. I still look back on that holiday today and the memories make me smile.

A few nights into the trip Robert suggested we head out together, just the two of us, for a few drinks and dinner before meeting up with the others. We found a beautiful, quiet authentic Spanish restaurant away from the madness of the main drag and ordered some food.

It was a lovely place and I found myself looking at Robert in a different light. He was a true gentleman. He was attentive. He remembered what I liked to eat and drink, he would always ask me about myself and he was genuinely interested in my life. John had been a lovely boy, Robert was a young man. A spark of attraction had begun to fizzle in my heart but rather than a bright flame, it was a warm glow. I was increasingly tactile with him. As we left the restaurant and walked back towards the main district I held his hand. I gave in to the moment and we kissed.

It happened so quickly and so naturally I had to catch my breath.

What just happened? I thought. We pulled apart shyly. We had just entered uncharted territory.

I didn't know what to say. I didn't know if I was doing the right thing and we sloped back to the rest of the group and said nothing. Throughout the evening I kept catching Robert's eye but I tried to stay calm and acted like nothing had happened. After a few drinks we returned to the bar in the complex. There was music on and I got up to dance with Robert. I gazed at him as we drew close.

Before I knew it, we were leaving and going back to Robert's room for a drink and a chat.

The thought of going to a bedroom with Robert left me with mixed feelings. While on the one hand I was a little excited by the idea, I was also nervous.

I hadn't slept with anyone since John and I wasn't sure that I was ready to get into a relationship. But I was getting swept along by the whole carefree holiday atmosphere.

In his room we started chatting.

The drink and the long day in the sun was beginning to take its toll.

'I haven't got any night clothes,' I said, but Robert had a blue Tommy Hilfiger shirt I could wear.

I went into the bathroom, slipped out of my dress, washed my make-up off and put on Robert's shirt. It smelled of him. We lay on the bed together, but all we did was talk and laugh the whole night. Nothing happened. It was really sweet.

I was falling for him and liked the way it felt. In the early hours of the morning we fell asleep side by side.

Late the next day there was no embarrassment when we woke. And after a cup of tea, we went to meet the others. There were a few knowing looks when we went down to the pool together. We spent the day dozing in the sun. We didn't mention our snog.

That night after getting ready I went down to the bar and Robert had already ordered me a gin and tonic.

I took a breath. 'I really enjoyed last night,' I told him.

It seemed like Robert had too and so when we got on to the subject of 'dating' properly I felt really pleased, but also a bit scared and embarrassed. I was shy. I couldn't help but be apprehensive too. I knew that if I entered into it a relationship with Robert, it was going to be a serious one. I hadn't felt like that about a man before.

'I need to think about things,' I said, not committing to anything. I didn't mean it to sound as if I was playing hard to get. I just needed to get my head around the whole scenario.

And with that we headed off into town and had a brilliant night. The more time I spent with Robert, the more I fell for him. I caught myself looking at him throughout the night. I was weighing up in my mind what to do but in the end I was led by my heart. At the end of the night I pulled Robert aside and I kissed him.

'I want to be your girlfriend,' I smiled.

It was official. Me and Robert were now a couple. I couldn't have been happier.

CHAPTER TEN

WHIRLWIND ROMANCE

For the last few days of the holiday we openly showed our affection and everyone was pleased for us and admitted they thought Robert had fancied me all along.

I joked that the holiday was just his ploy to get his wicked way with me. But nothing happened sexually until after we came back. I needed to be sure that Robert was the right one for me before I gave him my body as well as my heart.

I gradually began spending more time at his home. We both went back to work. I enjoyed spending time with Robert, it felt right. We had been such good friends before we made the romantic leap that we knew each other's likes, dislikes and habits.

Months passed. I wanted to look after Robert but my domestic skills were not great. I'd lived at home with Mum and Dad all my life and had always been looked after. I wasn't hopeless, I could clean and iron, but I wasn't a great cook. One Sunday morning in January we found ourselves in bed after a night out. We loved our lie-ins and we were both starving. I offered to make bacon sandwiches. I cremated them! The flat filled with smoke and the food was black round the edges.

After the ruined breakfast in bed Robert turned the hi-fi on and George Michael's song 'Heal the Pain' came through the speakers.

Robert started serenading me.

A blissful feeling of happiness washed through me. I was falling for him deeply and quickly.

When the song finished I had a lump in my throat. I took his face in my hands and kissed him gently on the lips.

'What are you doing next week?' he asked.

'I haven't got any plans,' I answered.

'Good,' he nodded. 'I am taking you to the Maldives for your twenty-first birthday, it's booked.'

Two weeks later I was on a jet to the Maldives to stay at the Hilton hotel where Katie Price and Peter Andre went years later – but I went there before them. We had the best time ever.

We were back in time for my twenty-first birthday and we had a party with all my friends in Romford. In the morning we woke up together and Robert took me for lunch in Smiths, a posh Essex restaurant. I'd had far too much to drink the previous night and regretted ordering the lobster almost immediately.

'I think I'm going to be sick,' I said feebly as I picked over the seafood.

Robert was understanding. He paid the bill and drove me home and put me to bed. Later on, when I was feeling better he came to see me while I was still in bed,

'I got you a birthday present,' he said, pulling a red box from his pocket and handing it to me.

'Robert,' I gasped, 'You didn't need to get me anything. You've already taken me to the Maldives.'

'It's just a little something,' he shrugged. It was the under-statement of the year. I ripped off the wrapper to reveal a Cartier box. I opened it excitedly and inside was a Tank Française, one of Cartier's most iconic watches. I screamed.

'I've got a Cartier. Oh my God!'

Robert swept me off my feet, he was wonderful.

Life turned into a whirlwind. I'd never travelled so much. I'd had holidays with the girls before but with Robert it was the Maldives and a few months later New York for Valentine's Day.

Ironically it was around that time that I was having money problems. I got offered my first credit card when I was eighteen. I was walking round Debenhams in London and a salesperson offered me an Abbey National Visa Platinum card. The credit limit was £4000. I had reached that within a few months. I had a lot of things to buy and the plastic allowed me to do it. It paid for a Cyprus holiday with the girls. We stayed in one of the top hotels in Ayia Napa. At the time, the thing to wear on the beach was Lancaster sunscreen and being from Essex I could not face the idea of being on the beach with Piz Buin so I spent hundreds on Lancaster products.

The limits on my card went up and up. Within a couple of years I had racked up £14,000 of debt. I got into that mess because I just didn't get it. I didn't get what money was about, I didn't understand it. I had always been given money by my dad. I was never taught about budgeting and I didn't have a clue about money management. The money went on clothes, holidays, meals, nights out. I had always had the best and when it came to standing on my own two feet I just thought that was what you did. You bought the best.

I realised I was in financial difficulty when the bills started to come through and I struggled to make the minimum payments. I never had to worry about bills before but I began to dread them.

When I had reached the credit limit on the Abbey National card I saw an ad for a Mint card offering a 0% balance transfer. I took the offer and for the next years I balance-transferred so many times that basically, I ran out of companies to use and I started to feel ill about it and realised I needed help. I turned to the person I had always turned to in times of crisis: my dad.

It took a while to pluck up the courage to tell him. Every time I steeled myself to broach the subject I found a reason not to. Finally, after family dinner one Sunday, I confessed all.

'I need some advice Dad,' I said. 'I've got some problems with credit cards.'

At first he was annoyed.

'How has this happened?' he said. 'How have you managed to spend that much money?' He was just as angry with the credit companies that allowed me to spend so much without any checks. He had never relied on credit cards and only spent what he could afford. He couldn't understand why people felt the need to live beyond their means.

'At some point you have always got to pay it back,' he sighed.

I had worked out that I would have to work fourteen months for nothing just to pay off the cards. As a sweetener to get me back on the financial straight and narrow Dad offered me a generous deal. He'd match the payments I made to get me back in the black sooner. I hugged him and vowed that I would not let him down. I worked hard and paid it all off.

When I was twenty-two my boss at the recruitment firm put me charge of my own agency: Superjobs. I took on a friend of mine, Alana, and we concocted a plan to make extra money. We would buy cheap denim shirts and customise them with the gold decorations and logos from fake Chanel earrings we bought from the market, then sell on the mock designer creations.

Soon after I got together with Robert I called Leah, John's friend, and we gossiped on the phone about my news.

'I'm made up for you Gemma,' she enthused. 'He sounds like a really lovely bloke. We must get together.'

And that's what we did. I felt nervous about introducing Robert to my ex's friend and wondered what Ben would make of him. For some reason their acceptance of my new man meant a lot to me. We arranged to meet at the Vojan restaurant in Ongar, one of my favourite curry houses. Leah and Ben were already there when we walked in. I hadn't seen them for many months and I got butterflies when I looked at Ben and saw that he hadn't changed. He was wearing a pink shirt and Leah was looking gorgeous as ever. I needn't have worried about Robert and Ben getting on. They clicked straight away and we laughed all night. After that first meeting Robert and Ben stayed in touch and became good friends for a while. But further down the road, Ben started to stay out late clubbing and partying. He had married at nineteen and he was getting itchy feet. Robert went with him a couple of times but I chose not to – it wasn't the life I wanted. Robert got bored of it very quickly as well and as friends we naturally drifted apart. We never fell out; we just went our own ways in life.

Robert's career in the City was going from strength to strength. He was regularly travelling abroad to meet clients and took me to a work event in Paris. I was living the high life. He flew me out first class and we stayed in a top city hotel near the Eiffel Tower.

On the second afternoon of the trip Robert said that there was a client lunch and that partners were invited. It was in an expensive French restaurant. I had packed a posh frock and Robert wore his best suit. The restaurant was in an amazing old building. The chandeliers that lit the main dining hall glittered with thousands of crystals. In the corner a string quartet played classical music. After a glass of champagne and canapés we were ushered to our seats and served caviar and steak tartare. Around the table everyone was talking about financial markets or making small talk, mainly about things they had bought. They discussed the pros and cons of new cars and talked about property prices. The women were mainly quiet. Eye candy, I thought to myself. I was happy to be there with Robert but bored at the same time. It was a taste of how the other half lived but it was a bit stuffy for my liking. I looked out the big windows at the front of the restaurant absent-mindedly. Then, out of the corner of my eye something caught my attention. It was the Christian Dior shop. I was drawn to the logo above the shop door. It was staring me in the face. It was sparkling. I stared at the bags in the window display and almost started to salivate. I had the Cartier watch, I wanted a Dior bag to go with it. I was like a big-game hunter stalking my next prey.

At that point in my life I had worked hard and my credit-card bill was almost clear. Dad had taught me well. I wanted a bag badly but I wasn't prepared to get into debt again for one. I did have another option however. When I was young, Dad, ever the practical parent, had taken out a savings plan for me. It matured when I was twenty-one and there was about £3000 in it. I had a card I could draw the money out on. I spent the rest of the lunch debating with myself whether it was prudent to spend my life savings on a handbag.

I knew it wasn't but I really, really wanted a Dior. I even convinced myself it would be an investment. It was like a piece of art, it would go up in value the older it got.

After we'd eaten I saw my chance and escaped. I found a cashpoint nearby, drew out a wad of Euros and practically skipped to the boutique. I thought I had died and gone to heaven. It was a lovely feeling, like a moment from a dream. I was in Paris in Christian Dior and I could afford to buy a bag. I still have that bag today. I won't part with it until the day I die. In honesty, apart from that spending spree when I was younger I don't treat myself too much. I didn't feel guilty about buying it. You only live once! I was living the Essex dream.

CHAPTER ELEVEN

HOME SWEET HOME

t's amazing how quickly time can fly when you are content. I had fallen hook, line and sinker for Robert. Conversation often turned to our living arrangements. I was spending most of my time at his flat so it soon became obvious that it would make sense to live there full-time. We agreed that Robert would buy a new place and I would move in with him.

'What do you reckon about these?' he asked, waving the papers in front of me. He had chosen several adverts of barn conversions in Essex . They all looked gorgeous. But the prices were eye-watering. He then pulled out another ad. PROPERTY AUCTION, REPOSSESSED PROPERTIES FOR SALE, it read.

Robert had done his homework. He knew that one of the lots at the auction that was taking place the following week was a barn conversion in the countryside. He showed me the picture of it from the brochure. It was stunning. There was no minimum and it was repossession so was bound to go for much less.

I started to feel a tingle of excitement.

A week later we sat anxiously holding each other's hand at a property auction. I'd never been to one before and didn't know what to expect. Before the auction started we went into a nearby pub and had a couple of drinks to steady our nerves.

The auction room was a real mix of people. There were couples like us hoping to bag a bargain, men in suits who I presumed were property investors and a few rougher looking men, who I thought were maybe builders looking for wrecks to do up and sell on. Luckily the property we were interested in was halfway through the auction so we got a chance to see how the system worked. It was simple enough. If you were interested in something, you raised your hand and indicated that you wanted to bid. Mostly the auctioneer dictated the price of the bid, so people didn't have to make decisions about how much they wanted to offer. The auctioneer would ask for a price, and if someone matched it he would increase it by a few thousand pounds and ask if anyone else was interested. If no one topped the last bid, the bidder walked away with the property. Some had reserve prices, others were going for a steal.

The brochure had full details of the property we were interested in and a range of colour photos. It looked amazing and I was soon swept up in the excitement of the sale. It didn't occur to me what would happen if someone bought the house they bid on but then went to see it and realised they didn't like it. It was a big commitment to make just from looking at pictures in a brochure.

Midway through the afternoon the barn conversion Robert had his eye on came up for bidding.

'Who will offer me £200,000?' barked the auctioneer.

Half the room raised their hands, including Robert.

The price rose rapidly, increasing in £10,000 multiples. It was getting down to the nitty-gritty and Robert had a determined look on his face.

The man he was bidding against shifted in his seat.

'The bid is with you sir,' the auctioneer said.

The man hesitated for several seconds. He was thinking. I squeezed Robert's arm. Surely the place was his.

Then he nodded. I felt Robert tense.

The auctioneer turned back to him once again. I watched open-mouthed as Robert made another bid and then the other man shook his head as the auctioneer came back to him.

Then the words that I'd only ever heard on *Bargain Hunt* came …

'Going once … going twice … going three times to the gentleman in the blue shirt.' The gavel came down on the wooden stand and Robert was the proud owner of a barn conversion that was going to be our new home.

I shrieked.

'I can't believe you just bought that,' I said cuddling him.

He let out a long breath and grinned. His cheeks were flushed from the adrenaline rush he'd just been on.

There was paperwork to fill out and while Robert was going through the formalities I went to wait in the pub next door. He came out the auction house beaming and holding a set of keys.

I couldn't quite believe what was happening as we drove the short distance to the outskirts of Billericay. The area had a village feel to it and the house was down a country lane.

We pulled up in the drive and I gasped. The house was stunning; it was a dream home. It had a sweeping staircase and a massive kitchen with a double range oven. The downstairs had a huge lounge with an open fire. Upstairs there were four bedrooms, all of them with en suite bathrooms.

The house was set in beautifully manicured gardens and was bordered by fields at the back. The previous owner had planted rose bushes around the place.

'It's perfect,' I breathed.

Robert moved in bit by bit over the following weeks. There were a few jobs to do in the house and a bit of decorating and he wanted to make sure it was perfect before he moved out of his flat permanently. I moved my things in too, which were mainly clothes. There was plenty of space to store it all.

The house became my pride and joy over the following months. The rose bushes burst into flower, lining the driveway with pink blooms. I took good care of them and employed a gardener to come and mow the lawn and do the gardening every couple of weeks. We invited friends round most weekends and I got good at cooking. Every Sunday we would invite our families round for a roast, which I lovingly cooked in the range. Christmas came and we hosted mince-pie and wine parties for the people we knew. I made friends with the shopkeepers in the high street and knew them all by name. We bought furniture together. We ordered a sofa from DFS to replace the old one Robert had brought with him.

But while Robert bought most of the stuff I never took him for granted and he never let me. For the first year we were there the house was a work in progress. One evening we were discussing what curtains to get.

'I saw some lovely drapes in a boutique in Chigwell,' I said. 'We should get those.'

They were extremely expensive.

But Robert wasn't the type of person who would just walk in with a new Rolex watch or a Cartier bracelet. He treated me but he didn't spoil me. There is a difference. I had a lovely life with him. We went to the best restaurants and stayed in the best hotels. Robert sorted everything out. I wasn't earning as much as him and couldn't contribute as much but I made sure I got the shopping. He wasn't a pushover and although he was very generous and would think nothing of splashing out on a luxury holiday, he often drew the line. I decided to save up for those curtains myself and in the meantime had plain linen drapes up in the lounge from Ikea. Because of my family background it didn't bother me to wait for the nice things in life. I would rather live in a two-bedroom flat with quality stuff rather than stay in a big house furnished with tat.

I had always wanted a man who would look after me but never expected to be looked after financially. I have always worked and always expected to pay my way. The thing I really craved was strong support from a man because I had always had that in my life growing up, and Robert provided that.

Robert filled the role and every day was a holiday with him for the first two years we were together.

Basically, he was always there and he was loyal and dependable. My parents thought a lot of him. He spent a lot of time at our house and they looked at him a bit like a surrogate son. They were pleased when we got together. They knew he was a decent chap. They were pleased that I had settled with someone who was looking after me and who had a good job and a promising future.

I was still young and I had a lot of responsibility for the house. I was working hard and then coming home and cooking for us. I wanted to look after my man. At the weekends when all my friends were going out or arranging girlie holidays, I was playing the domestic goddess. I loved cookbooks and I loved going out and buying knick-knacks for the house. I was making a home for us. I was more into buying CIF and going to Ikea than I was into going clubbing. I grew up quickly. I didn't feel that I was getting old before my time but I felt that my life had become very different in a short space of time.

I was living in the house of my dreams with the man who had swept me off my feet. We were in love. We had a blissful life together. While my friends were out living their youth, I was doing the cleaning and cooking. And as the months rolled by I kept hearing a little niggle in the back of my mind. It was my mum's voice from years ago.

'Be careful what you wish for,' she was warning.

CHAPTER TWELVE

DON JUAN

've often tried to unravel where it started to go wrong. The funny thing was that we never argued. We always got on well with each other. But after two years I began to feel like my domestic bliss had become a prison. There was a gradual change. We started out doing everything together but Robert was getting busier and busier at work. He was getting more responsibility and doing longer hours. The work started to encroach on our time together. I understood. Robert's job was his life, he was paid well and his job provided us with the luxuries we had. So I understood on the countless occasions he would call and apologise because he was staying late in the office or meeting clients.

And, at first, when the meetings extended into the weekend I accepted that it was part of his job. And when he went off to play golf on Sundays I knew it was his way of unwinding.

I could sense we were getting distant. I was left to my own devices. I was in the barn on my own a lot (I'd started calling it the barn because it felt big and empty most of the time); I had time on my hands to assess the situation. I started to wonder if the life I found myself in was really the life I wanted. I felt down, I had a niggling feeling that my life was heading in the wrong direction. I got depressed.

We still went out. Robert was still extravagant and took me to lovely places. We had a holiday in Barbados and he took me to the top restaurants in London. He educated me in fine dining and fine wines but I was young and I would have been happy with a bottle of Black Tower if it meant we could laugh and be carefree like we had been in the early days of our relationship. The nights out and laughs became few and far between and my life was punctuated by work and long lonely days and nights locked away in my dream home. I started to feel that my youth was being taken away from me. I was still young but I was living the life of a dutiful wife. I resolved that I needed to get out more.

Around that time one of the best places to go on the Essex social scene was the Friday-night disco in a local hotel. All sorts used to go on the nightclub. It was a bit of a meat market. Often there would be over 600 people in it, most of them looking for someone to take to one of the rooms for the night. But it was a laugh and it was the place to be seen. A few of my friends were regulars and I decided that I would tag along with them one night when Robert was working late. He often went for a drink with colleagues after he'd worked late on Friday so there was no point me staying at home waiting for him. I wanted to have a little fun.

The first night I went it was buzzing. I wore skintight Lycra trousers and a tight black top. The place was heaving and people had made a real effort. There was a lot of glamour packed into a small area. There was a big age range of people there and quite a few older men and women. A lot of people seemed to know each other. I grabbed a vodka, lime and soda and had a look round to take in the surroundings. I felt a little apprehensive to begin with. I had become so used to going places with Robert that being there without him felt alien. I found myself wishing he would walk through the door and take me away. I missed him but I knew he was in the City somewhere talking currency exchange with his office buddies.

In one corner there was a group of older guys. They all looked like proper geezers in sharp clothes with big watches dripping off their wrists. One bloke in particular looked very suave. He had Armani jeans on, a Ralph Lauren striped shirt and a black blazer over the top. He caught me looking at him and winked. I looked away, embarrassed. That night I had a surprise. Cassie, Louise and their mum walked in. We hadn't been in touch for several years, since I left Frances Bardsley, and at first I was a little apprehensive. But that time in my life seemed so far away it almost seemed like it had never happened. I had grown up a lot since then; in fact, given my domestic circumstances, I felt practically middle-aged. Cassie and Louise had grown up too. I decided to go over to them and say hello.

'Gemma?' Louise asked when I tapped her on the shoulder. 'Oh my God, it's been years.'

She was genuinely pleased to see me and I was just as pleased to see her. We had a few drinks and laughed about old times. It was lovely to see Louise and her sister again and at the end of the night we promised to stay in touch.

'I can't believe we ever lost touch. So silly,' I said. The sisters nodded and we all exchanged numbers.

I didn't have to wait long to meet up again. A week later Cassie, who was single at the time, called and we arranged to meet up. By that time Robert was busy most weekends, so I rekindled my friendship with her and we started going out regularly on Friday nights. My old school friends Kelly and Vicky would come along too.

One of our regular haunts was a pub that was very much part of the Friday-night Essex social pub and club crawl. People would meet there, have a few drinks and then head to a club later.

A few weeks after I saw Cassie, I was out with Kelly and Vicky when an older guy walked up to me, bold as brass and said: 'All right princess? Can I get you a drink?'

I recognised him as the man whose eye I had inadvertently caught a few weeks previously. He had a lot of front and a big character. I could hardly say no. He had a huge cheeky smile on his face and bucketloads of confidence.

'Go on then, I'll have a brandy on the rocks,' I said.

He clicked his fingers and whistled at the bar staff, got served ahead of the other drinkers who had been queuing before him and handed me my drink.

'So what's your name then princess?' he asked.

I told him and we started to chat. His friends came over and joined us and they all had me and the girls in stitches. They were all car dealers from Essex.

Because of what happened next, I will call the man who was chatting me up Don Juan.

'Are you coming to the club later?' he asked.

He was tall, dark and had thick hair. I fancied him, I went for older men. I glanced at his hand and he wasn't wearing a ring.

'Yeah, we weare leaving in a bit,' I said. I told him the name of the club and we arranged to meet.

The club was packed but Don Juan and his gang had their corner. It was as if that part of the club was reserved for them. I played cool and didn't go over to him. Let him come to me, I thought.

I could feel him looking at me as I chatted to Vicky and Kelly and a short while later I felt a warm hand on the small of my back. I turned and there he was holding a drink for me.

'You look thirsty,' he smiled.

He was up for a laugh and that night we danced and chatted.

As midnight rolled around I told him I was going to head off and that it had been good to meet him.

'Do you want a lift home?' he offered. 'I wasn't going to stay much longer anyway.'

I didn't fancy having to wait in line for a taxi so the offer was gratefully accepted. We left the club and Don Juan led me to his BMW.

'Nice motor,' I said, as I climbed in.

I knew Robert wouldn't be back until the early hours so it wasn't as if I would have to explain myself. And Don Juan had been a gentleman all night. I knew instinctively that he wasn't the type of man who would try it on with me.

We pulled up at the end of the lane where I lived and I said my goodbyes and thanked him for the lift.

As I climbed out he caught my arm.

'You're a Dolly Daydream you are,' he said. And with that I walked off up the lane, smiling to myself. I had been starved of attention for months and months. I had begun to feel that I was no longer attractive. That compliment was like a breath of fresh air, like a drug. I was hooked. I found myself thinking about Don Juan for the rest of the weekend and spent hours at my desk that week daydreaming and wondering if we would meet again.

Things moved quickly. The following week Robert was away on a business trip and I was in Romford shopping. I bumped into an old friend of mine who knew Don Juan. We had spoken about her when we were chatting and realised we both knew her. She told me that he had been in touch with her asking for my number and asked if she could give it to him.

'Why not?' I said.

That afternoon my phone rang with an unrecognised number. I usually screen calls I don't know but intuition told me to answer.

'Is that my Dolly Daydream?' asked the voice at the other end of the line in a thick Essex accent.

We talked briefly and Don Juan asked me to go for a drink with him that night. A pulse of excitement shot through me. I felt as if I was standing on the edge of something and that, if I agreed, I might not like where I would end up. I was in a relationship with Robert, Don Juan was larger than life, he was much older than I was and I got the impression that he wasn't looking for long-term love. But I needed to feel wanted and attractive and I agreed, as long as I could bring a friend. I didn't want him to get the idea that it was a date.

When I put the phone down my heart was racing. Prickles of sweat had popped out on my top lip. What had I done? But it was too late to back down and I convinced myself that it was just a bit of innocent fun. I rushed out and bought a new outfit, which consisted of jeans and a halter-neck top from Oasis with a zip at the back and red and pink roses on it. I booked in for an emergency hair appointment and dug out a pair of pink Barbie-style heels with a bow on the front to complete the outfit. Casual but glam was the look I was going for.

We had arranged to meet at a pub in Romford. I'd describe it as a rough diamond as back then it was quite rough.

'It's a dive,' my friend groaned when our cab pulled up outside.

I was 45 minutes late on purpose but he never even mentioned it. He was there with his friends and as I walked in and saw him I caught my breath. He looked lovely. He was wearing a cardigan with jeans and a shirt. The sleeves were slightly rolled up to show off his Rolex. There was a manliness about him that I couldn't resist. I knew I was going to be safe when I was with him. Throughout my life I had always looked for that older man, someone like my dad, and Don Juan looked like he fitted the mould. He had the banter, he was funny and he could look after me.

We had a great laugh that night and later in the evening conversation turned personal.

'So are you single?' I asked.

'I'm just going through a divorce,' he replied. 'What about you?'

'I'm seeing someone but it's not serious,' I lied.

That night we shared a ride home and when I went to get out Don Juan leaned across to give me a kiss goodbye. It was one of those awkward 'lips or cheek' moments. We both chose the lips and swapped saliva in the back of a black cab.

'I'll see you again,' he said when we pulled ourselves away from each other.

'You will,' I winked. Robert was the furthest thing from my mind. I was on cloud nine.

Robert came back from his work trip and things continued as normal. We were hardly speaking and living separate lives. The fun and laughter had drained from our relationship. On Saturdays Robert would watch television in the lounge while I was in the kitchen listening to Stevie Wonder songs and living for Friday nights when I'd see Don Juan. It became a pattern for about a month. Every Friday, Robert would be out with his mates after working late and I would go to meet my fancy man and his crew. We would sometimes go to a pub or for a meal first. His social circle was full of characters. I had never experienced that sort of dangerous, dodgy-dealing lifestyle before. There was no glamour, there were dodgy pubs and bars, but I was with great people: the duckers and divers, the proper Essex geezers. I was seeing what life was about. It was a shock to me but it was also an adrenaline rush. They were a world away from the kind of people I had known. It was entertainment, they were selling fake Rolexes and drinking LPR Rose, it was all fur coat and no knickers with them but it was exciting.

It was like a flirtation and I knew it was wrong, but it was the only thing that brightened the dull days of loneliness. I was living a fantasy. I was young and silly. I dreamed about being with him. He only had to look at me and call me Dolly Daydream and I melted. Don Juan was my escapism. I was hooked on the excitement and the thrill of the chase.

I almost got caught one Sunday. I was in the kitchen cooking Robert a roast dinner. While I was chopping the carrots my phone rang. I'd left it in the lounge. Robert often picked up my calls. I panicked. What if it was Don Juan and Robert answered? I threw down the knife and raced into the lounge just as Robert huffed and got up off the sofa to get my phone.

I grabbed it before he did. Don Juan' number was displayed on the screen.

'Wrong number,' I shrugged, cutting off the call.

The excitement that rushed through me was unbelievable. Outside of Friday nights we rarely spoke. I wanted to speak to him. I made an excuse that I had forgotten the gravy and needed to pop to the shops. I then quickly got in my car and drove round the corner to speak to Don Juan, who invited me out for a drink.

'Sorry, I've got the family over to dinner,' I said. I was gutted.

Don Juan never pushed me for anything more. We met, we had a laugh and we had a snog. I had fallen for him but I knew I was never going to cross that line with him and be intimate with him. Sex wasn't on the agenda.

As the weeks went on I began to wonder where my dalliance with Don Juan was leading. I had to admit to myself that it was going nowhere and that if I wanted things to work out with Robert, I needed to cut my fancy man loose. Perhaps I was growing up. One weekend I was out again and Robert was away. For the first time in a long time I found myself missing him and thinking about the fun we used to have.

'This isn't for me, none of it,' I said to myself as I looked around at the throng of clubbers. I walked out of the club that night and I didn't go back. There were no calls from Don Juan. I realised he was probably just as realistic as me. It was a bit of fun and lovely while it lasted.

Some time later I heard on the grapevine that Don Juan had been arrested. He had been caught drug dealingand was waiting to go to trial. I was horrified. He had never spoken about drugs to me and although he was a wheeler and a dealer, I never had him down as a drug pusher. I was shocked. I am really anti-drugs, they ruin lives, but part of me felt sorry for him. How had he got himself caught up such a serious offence? How would he cope in prison? But he was smart, he would be able to look after himself. I didn't think I'd ever see him again but a few weeks later I was in a bar in Romford and I saw some of Don Juan's crew. I went over to say hello to them.

'Can you tell him I said hello and that I'm thinking of him' I said.

'Tell him yourself love,' said one of them. 'He's coming here in a minute. It's his last night out on bail before the trial. He's going to plead guilty so he'll be gone for a long time.'

My heart skipped a beat and when he walked in half an hour later it was like a scene from the movies. There was no one else in that bar except him and me. The music was pumping but I couldn't hear; all I could hear was the blood pumping in my ears. He walked through the crowd with his trademark confidence and swagger and to me it looked as if he was walking in slow motion. I wanted to drink him in. He was wearing a navy blue blazer and looked gorgeous.

When he spotted me his face lit up.

We hugged and held the embrace.

We chatted for a while but I didn't mention the case. When it was time to go I had a heavy feeling in my stomach. I knew it was goodbye.

I took his hand.

'I'm sorry about what has happened,' I told him. 'I will never forget you.' I was welling up with emotion.

He smiled kindly.

'Just get on with your life Dolly Daydream,' he said. And that was it. I turned and left, Don Juan went to trial and got sent down. I never saw him again. True to my word I have never forgotten him. I often think about him now and reminisce about the fun times we had together and I would love to see him again.

With Don Juan on a long holiday courtesy of Her Majesty I knew I had to do something about Robert and me. We had been living in limbo for too long and we needed to sort ourselves out or go our separate ways.

I resolved to tell Robert how I felt. If we were going to salvage our relationship we needed to start talking.

I arranged for us to go out for a Chinese meal on a Saturday night.

'Are you happy with the way things are going Robert?' I asked. 'Be honest with me.'

As Robert looked up from his spare ribs, I knew in my heart-of-hearts it wasn't working for either of us.

'I'm really down about it Robert, I feel lonely. We've got ourselves in a bit of a rut,' I said.

Robert agreed and by the end of the meal, we'd vowed to try harder and make our relationship work. I bit down on my fortune cookie with a renewed spirit. I loved Robert and I was sure we were meant to be.

It was the start of 2004. I turned twenty-three and our New Year's resolution was to spend more time together. It began to work. We had meals out and we started to plan things.

A few months previously I had changed jobs. I was now working on reception at a local BMW dealership. I had left recruitment and been temping in banks in the City but Robert had suggested I get a job nearer home so I didn't have the hassle of commuting. I was around more and Robert made sure he didn't do so many late nights.

The passion and love started to filter back into our relationship. As spring came I started to feel that we had turned things round. I was optimistic for the future.

As April came we planned a holiday; the first we had thought about for a long time as Robert had been too busy for much of the previous year. We booked to go to Barbados in August. As Easter approached I started to feel unwell. I had a stomach bug that wouldn't seem to shift. I kept suffering from waves of nausea and felt tired all the time. I went to the doctor and was told I had a stomach virus and was given tablets.

But the illness didn't shift and after a couple of weeks I was getting worried that something was seriously wrong with me.

As Easter weekend came I vowed to go back to the doctor after the holidays and get referred to a specialist. We had planned a big roast at the house for the family on the Bank Holiday Monday and the day before Robert decided to get in a round of golf as the weather was warm and bright. That evening we were going out for dinner with some of Robert's friends and their partners and I popped to Tesco to get a few bits and pieces for the following day. My stomach was still sore and I had begun to suffer from uncomfortable heartburn along with the nausea. While I was in the supermarket I went to the pharmacy section to get some Pepto Bismol, I'd started drinking a lot of the stuff to get rid of the burning in my chest. I believe there were spirit guides or angels with me that day because while I was looking for the medication on the shelves a pregnancy test fell on the floor by my feet.

I looked at it and a thought popped into my head. When did I have my last period?

'Fuck!' I breathed quietly. I thought hard but I couldn't remember. It must have been months before. 'I am pregnant,' I thought to myself. The realisation hit me like a hammer blow. I had to know there and then, I couldn't wait. I picked the test up from the floor and bought it.

I didn't want to go into the toilets and do it because I didn't want to be on my own if it was positive. Hazel lived the closest so I drove to her house and knocked on her door. I often popped in unannounced so she wasn't surprised when I turned up clutching a Tesco carrier bag.

'Thought I'd pop in for a cuppa,' I said casually. She was doing her washing and was pleased to see me. She ushered me in.

'Can I use your loo?' I asked.

While she was folding her sheets in the utility room I scurried into her downstairs toilet and read the instructions on the back of the box. A blue line meant I was pregnant. I convinced myself I was being silly and that I just had a stomach bug as I peed on the stick and waited. It seemed like an eternity and to begin with I couldn't make out whether there was a line appearing in the window on the plastic stick or whether my eyes were playing tricks on me. But after two minutes there was no doubt. A thick blue line had appeared. The test was positive. I was having a baby. The shock hit me straight away. When I stood up my legs were shaking.

I walked in to Hazel. She took one look at me and a frown creased her forehead.

'What's wrong Gemma?' she asked. Instinctively she stepped towards me and held me. She could see I was distressed.

'I'm pregnant.' I repeated it over and over again. My whole body was shaking by then. Powerful emotions swept through me. What was I going to do? I wasn't happy, I wasn't sad. I was scared and confused. We hadn't planned it and we hadn't ever talked seriously about having children. I wondered what my parents would say. I was still so young; I had so much to do with my life. I started to sob uncontrollably.

Hazel soothed me.

'It's OK, Gemma,' she said. 'It's a good thing. It's brilliant news.'

But I wasn't convinced. It was a life-changing event and the thing that worried me the most was how Robert would react. We'd only just got our relationship back on track.

'Come on Gemma, pull yourself together now,' said Hazel after a while. She sat me down at the breakfast bar and made me a cup of tea.

'I don't know what to do,' I sniffed.

'At the moment love, you don't do anything. You're bound to be in shock. It's a natural reaction. You don't have to make any decisions about anything right now. You've got plenty of time to do that over the coming weeks. You need to speak to Robert first.'

I was also worried because I had been on medication for my stomach while I was pregnant. I wondered what effect that would have had. I had been on the pill and was racking my brain to work out how it had happened. Maybe I'd missed one. Maybe I wasn't as far along as I thought and had had a stomach bug after all and been sick one morning after I took a pill? It didn't change anything though.

I stayed with Hazel for an hour to get my head straight and when I felt strong enough hugged her goodbye, put the test in my handbag and went off to tell Robert.

I had always wanted children – even now the happiest day of my life will be when my children are sitting with me in my favourite Italian restaurant, the Bel Sit, having dinner. That's when I will know I have cracked it, when I have my kids and a husband. But back then I didn't know if I was ready.

I picked Robert up from golf. He could see I was in a state.

'I'm pregnant,' I blurted out.

He inhaled deeply. His reaction was similar to mine. Shock, then not knowing how to feel but he said he would support me if I wanted to be a mother.

A wave of relief washed over me. It was what I wanted to hear.

That night we cancelled our arrangements and went to the Mandarin Palace, a Chinese restaurant in Hornchurch and talked more. The shock was wearing off and with Robert's support I was beginning to get used to the idea. We wanted the baby. We wanted to be parents and to take our relationship to another level.

We went home and climbed into bed and spoke about baby names.

'If it's a girl I want to call her Dolce Bella,' I said.

Robert wanted something plain like Sarah.

'No, it'll be either Angel, Summer or Dolce Bella.' I knew it was a girl, I had intuition. That night we also told Mum and Dad and went for a meal with them the following evening.

At first they were as shocked as we had been.

'How did it happen?' Mum asked.

'Do you want me to draw a diagram?' I joked. When they could see that we were happy with the situation, though, they were too. Robert and I were going to be parents.

CHAPTER THIRTEEN

AT ROCK BOTTOM

The next days were bliss. After the initial shock we started to make plans for the future. It all began to feel right. I had been with Robert several years. We had a house, we had money and we would give our baby a loving, secure life.

After a week, the realisation of what was happening had properly set in. It was then that I started to sense things were not as rosy as I hoped. The initial excitement seemed to disappear. At first I hoped it would just take time for us to adjust to the idea.

'It's natural to be uncertain,' I told myself. 'It's a big change.'

But then when I spoke to Robert the truth became clear.

We didn't argue. We talked it through and the discussions continued throughout the day. I began to question everything about my life. Was I too young? There was still so much I wanted to do and a child would make it difficult. I started to have doubts too and I didn't want to raise a child that wasn't going to be wanted by both parents.

I spoke to Mum about it.

'If he's not sure and you go ahead I wonder whether he'll stick around and you'll be a single parent. Is that what you want?' she asked.

The thought of raising a child on my own scared me. At the time I was earning £16,000 a year as a receptionist at BMW. It would be a massive struggle. I didn't know what to do. Within days my dream of domestic bliss had turned to a nightmare.

Time was moving on and I needed to make a decision. I didn't know how many months pregnant I was and I made an appointment at a local clinic for a check-up.

I was examined and told I was around three months pregnant. I was shocked because that would mean I had continued to take the pill after I had conceived. I asked the doctor whether this would have an effect on the baby.

'It's not ideal,' he said, 'further tests will clarify things.'

He asked if I had taken any other medication. I explained that I had been given tablets for a suspected stomach problem early in the pregnancy.

Again he was concerned.

'It is very possible that the embryo could be affected,' he told me.

I didn't know what to do. I was completely confused and full of doubt. The doctor couldn't tell me any more without tests, which he said would be invasive and might also be problematic at such an early stage in the pregnancy. He suggested that I see a specialist. I walked away from the clinic in disarray. My emotions were all over the place.

In the following days I had three different opinions from other specialist birth units in London. They all said I might have damaged the baby and that it might have birth defects. They could not say for sure but advised that the baby might not necessarily be healthy. The consensus opinion was that the probability of complications was high.

With these doubts at the forefront of my mind I did something I am not proud of but which I felt at the time was my best and only option. I booked into a clinic for an abortion. It was the most difficult decision I have ever made in my life and I was numb in the days leading up to my appointment.

When the day came to go through with the termination I could barely get out of bed. I was trying hard to keep it all together. It's for the best, I kept telling myself and in my head I knew it was. It was just that my heart was aching. There was a deeper issue. I knew that after the procedure I needed to think long and hard about Robert and me.

Robert came with me but when I walked into the clinic I started to shake. My heart was pounding. I was scared.

'I don't think I can go through with this,' I told him.

I couldn't hold back the emotional tsunami that was crashing through me and I broke down weeping in reception.

'I can't do it,' I sobbed and I walked out.

I was in too much of a state to go through with it. We got in the car and when I had calmed down we went to the Bel Sit restaurant. It was one of the places that made me happy. I needed to be in familiar surroundings.

I ordered a glass of red wine but couldn't drink it. We ate in silence.

I felt worthless. We got in the car and drove home in silence. We walked through the front door. Robert went in the living room and I went upstairs. We didn't speak for the rest of the afternoon. The atmosphere in the house was tense. I craved understanding but felt alone.

The next morning when I woke I knew I had no future with Robert. I was on my own. I took deep breaths to try and calm the panic in my mind. I had to get through the crisis and the only person I could rely on was me. I shut the rest of the world out. I didn't think to turn to my parents or my friends. I didn't want to bother anyone with my problems. I put on my mental armour and tried to numb myself to the task I believed I had to do.

Robert got up and went to work and so did I. I made another appointment at the clinic and a few days later I went – on my own.

The procedure had to be carried out under general anaesthetic and up until the point where I was being put under I managed to keep my nerves at bay. As I was going under my heart started racing and the thoughts that I had been trying to keep silent burst through. I needed to walk away from Robert, I was having a termination, my dream life was over; it wasn't how my life was supposed to be.

When I came round I was groggy and confused. It took a while for me to focus and realise where I was and what had happened. I was lying in a recovery room on my own. Outside I could hear the muted sounds of the clinic: nurses were talking to patients, phones were ringing, medical machinery was beeping. A kind nurse came in and checked my heart rate, temperature and blood pressure.

'It's all done now,' she said. 'Everything went to plan, no complications.'

I felt terrible. I lay in bed for several hours feeling numb. I was emotionally exhausted but I knew I had to be strong.

For the next two weeks I tried to be positive and I tried to find a way to salvage my relationship. When I told Robert I had been to the clinic and had the termination he tried to be supportive. I told my parents and they were supportive too. I put on a brave face but deep down I couldn't shake the feeling of despondency that was eating away at me. I went back to work and acted as normal.

Then one day Robert and I had a row. I can't remember what it was about – at that point any little niggle would set us off. I was in the middle of cooking dinner and when Robert left the kitchen something in me snapped. The only way I can describe it is that I had built a psychological dam around my feelings to keep them contained. Normally the dam would keep them at bay. If I had a bad day I would struggle through and put problems to the back of my mind. I didn't deal with them. I stored them away and hoped the dam would hold. But this particular day the dam cracked and in the kitchen over a saucepan of spag bol all those negative feelings came pouring out.

I couldn't hold back the tears. I wept and let waves of tremendous grief wash over me. I was grieving for my baby and for my relationship. I couldn't understand how everything that had been so right was turning out so wrong.

Then I saw the knife rack and a strange feeling of clarity came over me. I knew how to make things better. I took a knife out and placed the cold steel blade on my hand. I pressed down hard and watched in fascination as the tip of the knife pierced my skin. The pain felt good. I drew the knife down and watched as a thin red line of blood sprang from the cut I had made. I withdrew the knife and repeated the action on a different part of my hand. Every time I cut my hand it was like a release. It felt good. Blood was tricking down on to the work surface.

Robert came in the kitchen and saw what I was doing. A look of horror spread across his face.

'What the ...?' he shouted at me. He ran over and took the knife from my hand. All I wanted was for him to put his arms around me and tell me everything would be all right.

I snapped out of the trance-like state I was in. And then I felt scared by what I had done. I knew I was losing control and I needed to pull myself back from the brink. I didn't want to kill myself. With hindsight I believe I did it as a cry for help. It made me feel better. I tried to explain to Robert but he must have thought I was going mad.

I patched myself up with plasters and the next day I went back to work. One of my colleagues saw my hand and asked what had happened. I told her I was helping my boyfriend cut back the rose bushes in the garden and that I had cut myself on the thorns. In my lunch hour I went and got special plasters with silicone in them that stop scarring.

That incident scared me. I had always felt in control of my life, even at the low points, and I always had faith that things would get better. I told myself that the scars on my hand and the scars on my heart would heal with time and I started to make an effort to go out and surround myself with friends and the positive people in my life.

It started to work. Over the next weeks I could feel myself getting stronger. I started going out on Friday nights with the girls and threw myself into work. Robert and I still were a long way off getting back on track. He had started to work late again but on most occasions it suited me as I was still wrestling with the idea that he was no longer the ideal man for me and that our relationship was fundamentally broken. One weekend he went away for a work event.

Rather than stay indoors I arranged to go to a place called the V Bar in Hornchurch with a friend. The bar was a well-known Essex nightspot and was tucked behind our favourite Chinese restaurant, the Mandarin Palace. I had been there many times in the past and had turned to my old haunts to make me feel better. I went with my friend Steph. We were having a laugh and a few drinks. I'd given her my door keys, my purse and my phone to put in her bag and at around 11.30 p.m., while she was chatting to someone, I went to the loo. There was a queue and when I came back out ten minutes later I hunted around the bar but couldn't find Steph anywhere (I learned later she'd presumed I had gone to the club we were planning to go on to and went there to find me). As I was looking round I spied a familiar face. It was a guy who lived in another village but I would often bump into at the local shop and we would stop for a chat every now and then. He was around thirty-nine, good-looking for his age and he seemed very kind. He was in the bar with a group of male friends. I walked over and he recognised me straight away.

'I'm really sorry to bother you,' I said. 'But my friend has gone off with my purse and phone. I know it's cheeky, but is there any chance I can borrow a tenner off you for a cab home?'

He laughed.

'Of course you can darling,' he said. 'But why kill a good night? Stay and have a drink with us.'

I'd already had a few drinks and was in the party mood. It would have been a shame to end the night because of a misunderstanding with Steph so I gratefully accepted his offer and, an hour later when he suggested we go for a Chinese, I was happy to tag along.

He was good company and as I sat at the bar in the Mandarin Palace watching him tear into his spare ribs I caught myself thinking 'phwoar'.

At the end of the meal he called a cab and we climbed in the back seat together, laughing and shamelessly flirting. I had no intention of taking things any further. I knew if our paths crossed as they had in the past it would make things awkward to say the least. But it just felt good to have a bit of innocent attention and some male company.

The cab pulled up at the end of the lane where I lived.

'Thanks,' I said, 'I've had a great night. Next time I see you I'll pay you back for the cab.'

He'd had a few to drink as well and his hands had been wandering on the way home. I didn't mind, I batted them away playfully.

'You can pay me back now,' he said and with that he leaned across and locked lips with me. At first I was shocked, and for a split second I didn't respond. But then the booze, the sexy smell of his aftershave and the thrill of snogging a stranger in the back of a cab got the better of me and I returned his attention.

The cab driver looked in his rear-view mirror and tutted. We pulled apart laughed nervously and my neighbour paid up and got out with me.

He looked at me expectantly.

'You can't come in,' I panicked.

'It's OK, we can use the fields at the back,' he suggested.

We both staggered round the back of the house into the open fields beyond and he pulled me to the grass. I fell on top of him and we carried on where we had left off in the cab, snogging and fumbling in the dark. I felt like a teenager.

It went no further that night and we both giggled as we straightened ourselves up and headed back to the road.

'Will I see you again?' he asked as I headed up the lane towards my house.

'I'll see you around,' I winked.

I had no house keys so I had to climb through a window at the back of the kitchen that had luckily been left open. I was a dishevelled wreck when I looked in the mirror. My dress was grass-stained and I had bits of twigs and vegetation in my hair. I went to bed feeling tipsy and happier than I had done for a long time.

In the morning the realisation of what I had done hit me along with a sizeable hangover. I worried about seeing the man again. What would I say? More than anything it would be a huge embarrassment. There was chance every time I popped out for a pint of milk I'd have to stop and make polite conversation over the fruit and veg?

Escapades like that however were just sticking plasters to cover up my true feelings. I have always been the sort of person who buries my feelings and gets on with life. I was suppressing how I really felt. I was full of doubt and sadness. I was scared and confused. I knew Robert and I had no future but I was hanging on in the hope that things would magically turn around. I felt stressed and anxious.

Those feelings had to come out somehow. Eventually something had to give. It began with an itchy scalp. I went to bed one night and continually woke scratching my head. The feeling got progressively worse throughout the night and by morning it felt as if my head was on fire. No matter how much I scratched I couldn't ease the hot, itchy feeling. I washed my hair in cold water, which gave some relief, and went to work feeling exhausted.

A few hours later the pain started again. I sat at my desk in the showroom clawing at my head. Alarm bells really started to ring when I felt something wet and sticky drip slowly down the back of my neck. I pulled my fingers from the tangle of my hair and looked at my fingertips and they were wet. I gently ran my hand over my scalp and could feel blisters. I gasped and immediately went to see my boss to tell him what was happening.

He advised I go straight to the doctor and I arranged an emergency appointment.

'You have a nasty case of psoriasis of the scalp,' I was told. 'Have you been under much stress lately?'

I admitted I had. I was prescribed lotion and advised to keep my head cool. I spent the rest of the week at my desk with bags of frozen peas pressed against my head.

It took weeks to clear up and I had countless sleepless nights, waking with my head burning and itching. Scratching only gave momentary relief and if the sores burst they became painful and infected. I'd be sitting at work and pus would start running down my face. I didn't think things could get any worse.

One weekend in the middle of the outbreak Robert and I were invited to a party by a friend of mine, Carly. I couldn't do anything with my hair or wear make-up in case it aggravated my scalp. I felt a mess and the last thing I wanted to do was go out and pretend I was happy. I decided to stay at my parents' in my old bedroom instead. I felt safe and secure there. The house had a lovely warm feel to it and I welcomed the chance for a break. I had continued to look after Robert, cook and clean for him, and I needed the rest and to put some space between us.

Robert decided to go to the party on his own and that night I had a premonition. I went to sleep comfortably for the first time in ages. Robert had said he would call to make sure I was OK. I hadn't heard from him by the time I fell asleep and I woke at 2.30 a.m. and knew he had met someone. It was a strong feeling. My intuition told me. I didn't know the details. I just knew and I knew I had to find a way to break away from him.

It was obvious that our relationship was in trouble but Robert seemed more preoccupied with buying a new car. He found one for sale nearby, and one Saturday in July 2004 he asked me to drive with him and pick it up. He bought it from a girl called Michelle. He woke up and he had a spring in his step because he was excited about getting a new boy's toy and went downstairs to the room he used as a dressing room to shower and get ready. He left his phone by the bedside and as I was getting out of bed a text came through on it.

I felt an urge to check it. I never made a habit of looking at his phone, I trusted him, despite all the late nights and work trips. But I had a very uneasy feeling and nervously I picked up the handset and scrolled down to the new message.

'Just gone for a run,' it read. And it was from a girl called Michelle.

A sick feeling came over me. Was this proof he was cheating? Had I caught him? All those months of confusion and frustration came bubbling through and I flew down the stairs and confronted him as he was drying himself off.

'What's this text on your phone?' I accused, waving the handset in his face like a maniac. He took a step back and read it. He didn't flinch. He looked me straight in the eye.

'You are a silly girl Gemma,' he said. 'Michelle is the girl I am picking the car up from today.'

'Why is she telling you she's going for a run?' I demanded.

'In case I turn up early,' he suggested.

I decided I was being paranoid and it was nothing to worry about.

We went to pick up the car and nothing was mentioned about the text or the run.

Life carried on for a few weeks as normal and soon it was time to begin packing for our trip to Barbados. We had a wonderful holiday booked and even though I questioned whether it was right to go away with someone who didn't want a child with me, I needed a break and I was trying to save our relationship. I was hoping the holiday would help us.

On the Friday before we were due to jet off Robert woke up before me and got ready for work while I was in bed.

He came in the room and suggested we went out that evening and get into the holiday mood. I could feel my heart melting. Perhaps the holiday was a good idea after all.

As I lay on the bed the sun shone through the windows. I wanted to be with him and I allowed myself the hope that perhaps we were going through a temporary glitch and we would be back to our fairytale life after a couple of weeks on a beach in the Caribbean. As he went to leave he looked back at me, it was like he couldn't walk away.

I got up, fed my cat Twinkle, a stray that I had rescued, and went to work. I sat at my desk all morning thinking about what I was going to have to eat that night and what I was going to wear. I was looking forward to it. I had been confused and lonely inside for so long but that morning I could see a silver lining.

Robert called me up at 4 p.m. There was a pause. Then the thing that was clearly bothering him hit me. He told me that he didn't want to be with me anymore.

I was dazed. I felt like someone had just hit me. I tried calling him back but his phone went straight to voicemail. I tried his mobile but that was switched off. I couldn't compute what had happened. My brain couldn't process it. Then the panic set in. I started hyperventilating, I felt sick and confused. My whole world had just collapsed in the space of a few seconds. I left the desk and walked into the kitchen. My legs were shaking. I leaned against the work surface and slid down to the ground on my knees. The sobs came in waves, I tried to be quiet and to hold them back but I couldn't. One of the boys who worked on the sales team came in and saw me crouched on the floor in tears.

'What's wrong Gemma?' he asked. Through sobs I told him.

He told me to go home. I left work in a state of shock; mascara was smeared down my cheeks and my eyes were red and puffy. I tried calling Robert again but he wasn't answering. I was on autopilot. I needed to see him and to speak to him. I didn't know what to do. I even bought a bottle of gin on my way home but I couldn't touch it when I got in. Instead I lay on the sofa crying. I didn't call anyone. I didn't tell any anyone. I didn't want anyone to know. I just needed to speak to Robert.

I sat there until 1 a.m. when he eventually came in. I had cried so much my head was pounding and my eyes were bulging. I was exhausted.

Robert walked through the door and he looked upset. He explained that he had been out for a few drinks.

He came and put his arms around me. His touch felt so reassuring but I thought it was an empty gesture. We spoke about what had happened.

'I just want to know why,' I sniffed.

Robert stayed silent.

'I'm exhausted, I need to sleep,' I told him. I walked to the nearest bedroom, the one Robert used to get ready in; it didn't feel right getting in the bed we shared.

In the morning after a fitful sleep, Robert gave me a ray of hope when we discussed still going to Barbados as friends. I didn't want it to end and I was still thinking we could go and make things work. I thought Robert was just having a wobble after the pregnancy and the termination. It was Saturday and we agreed to go to the Mandarin Palace for dinner. I wanted to make a special effort so that day I got my hair done and went into Debenhams and bought a black Ben de Lisi off-the-shoulder dress with sparkles on it. I spent ages getting ready and when I came down the stairs Robert was waiting in the lounge.

I put on a brave face. I had bottled up my feelings all day and tried to be positive. I wanted us to have a good night. I wanted him to remember what a laugh we could have together.

But, the ride to the restaurant was uncomfortable. I was becoming more upset but desperate not to show it. Waves of anxiety and sadness kept rising in my chest and I struggled to push them back. I didn't want to cause a scene. I just wanted us to have a nice night together.

In the restaurant Robert ordered sea bass in spring onions, garlic and ginger. We had been to the restaurant so many times and it was full of memories. We had shared countless sea-bass dishes and as the food was put on the table I cracked. I burst out crying.

'What is going on here? We are not together but we are now in a Chinese eating sea bass and, suddenly, I don't understand why this is happening.'

My voice was raised.

'Why Robert. Why?'

Robert put down his chopsticks hurriedly. There were no good answers. He ushered me out of the restaurant. We left the food uneaten. I cried all the way home. Robert tried to say that it was for the best and that we would still be good friends. I wasn't listening.

When we got home we went to bed in separate bedrooms.

In the morning we tried to talk again. Robert was more reso-lute than ever and told me he would be going away to get his head straight and to give me space. He'd be gone for two weeks and that would give me time to move out the house, although I could take longer if I liked.

I was leaving the house I had helped make a home for us. I knew it wasn't mine and I hadn't paid the mortgage on it but I had still cleaned and maintained it for him. But I agreed.

Robert disappeared for several days and I asked Steph to come and stay with me while I tried to come to terms with what was happening. I tried to call him over the following days but his phone went straight to voicemail. One night I started to panic.

'What if he's depressed because of the baby and has done some-thing stupid?' I said to Steph.

She told me straight.

'I doubt it Gemma. You need to get away from him.'

On Wednesday he returned to pick up some clothes. He was going to Ibiza, he explained.

I took one look at him and knew something was up. He looked like he had a new lease of life. I was falling apart, I looked a mess. Robert on the other hand had a spring in his step.

He went to his room and got in the shower. I wanted to know what was happening. I checked his phone and found some texts.

I threw open the shower door.

'What the fuck is going on?' I shouted.

Robert saw the phone in my hand and looked horrified. He tried to grab it from me.

I ran from the room. I wanted to read all the texts properly so I could see what he'd been up to.

I was wearing a bright pink dressing gown with a pink satin hood and nothing on underneath and I ran out of the house down the lane.

Robert ran after me, pulling on a pair of white shorts as he went. He caught up and we had a stand-off in the field by the house. I squared up to him.

'Just tell me who she is,' I shouted.

The rope on my gown had come undone and it was flapping open. I was naked underneath. Cars passing on the road outside could see everything.

I threw his phone in a ditch and ran back indoors while he tried to retrieve it. I changed tack and thought I would get his passport and put that down the drain. I ran back to the house, got his passport and ran outside. He came after me covered in mud. I dangled his passport over the drain.

'Not knowing is killing me Robert. Tell me who it is and you can have your passport back.'

Again he told me I was being paranoid. We were both panting.

What could I do? What would flushing his passport away achieve? I was kidding myself. I knew it was over and in that moment I knew I had to move on. Life as I had known it was over. I needed to get away from the place that I made my home and away from the man I loved.

I dropped his passport on the ground and walked indoors. Robert came in and cleaned himself up. He packed his bags and left.

I wallowed in bed for the next three days, then I started the painful process of packing. I spoke to Mum and Dad; they were sympathetic but glad I was getting out.

'He wasn't for you Gem,' Mum said.

As I packed I played Whitney Houston's 'Step by Step'. The lyrics about being strong in the face of adversity gave me strength. I left a week after our last bust-up. I took all the knick-knacks and things I had bought that had made the place a home. All I left for Robert was an old card he had given me and propped up by it I left the pregnancy test I had done a few months before. I closed the door behind me and tried to swallow back the tears that were pouring down my cheeks.

CHAPTER FOURTEEN

DARK DAYS

t was August, my favourite season in Essex. The sun was shining and if you knew the right crowd there was a pool party to attend every weekend. The streets were full of wide boys in soft-top cars. I wasn't interested in any of it. A black cloud followed me everywhere. My dream was over. I was back where I started from with my mum and dad and my heart had been shattered into a million tiny pieces. I was pining. Each day I would wake and go through the motions but the pain inside was unbearable. I wanted so much to get on with my life and to forget Robert but I felt I had no closure. The uncertainty as to why Robert had really left me ate me up. I still wondered if there would be a chance for us and it took all my willpower not to contact him.

I started having anxiety attacks. I would wake up in the middle of the night sweating. I had vivid, cruel dreams in which I was still living in the barn and Robert was asleep beside me. I would wake and reach over for him, and then as the fog of sleep lifted I would realise where I was and the tears would come.

Mum and Dad were fantastic. They were supportive and gave me space but they didn't indulge me and encouraged me to get on with life. I went from a four-bedroom house to the bedroom I had grown up in. Poor Mum must have had a heart attack when she realised how many clothes I was coming back home with. Nothing had changed in their house, my bedroom was the same as it was when I left. It was comforting – it still had my smell. Mum and Dad offered to decorate the room for me but I preferred it as it was. I clung to them for comfort. Every Friday night I would go out to dinner with them like the old days. We'd usually go to the local Indian restaurant, the Vojan in Ongar. They almost became my substitute boyfriend; I was with them all the time and I enjoyed it.

I started to find comfort in food. It became my friend and my coping mechanism. Takeaways became my social life. Every time I felt sad or anxious I would eat. I would treat myself to chocolate or ice cream. Food was an escape. I started to numb my true feelings with it. I was self-medicating with calories. Every time I felt an emotion I would eat to block it. Eating a bar of chocolate would make me feel momentarily happy and comforted. I was comfort-eating but at the time I just thought I was treating myself. Food gave me a high. I had always been slim so I never felt guilty.

There were days where I binged, never to the point where I made myself sick, but I would stuff my face. It wasn't unusual for me to have three bars of chocolate consecutively and then go to McDonald's and eat a Big Mac and a chicken sandwich.

I started to fixate about food. It became a focus away from the grim reality of my situation. I would think about it from the minute I woke to the minute I went to bed. I had low self-esteem. I was suffering and without realising I morphed into a bigger person. I went from being a thin girl who never had a weight problem and was a constant size 10 to a girl who couldn't stop growing. I went to a 12, then to a 14, a 16 and an 18 within a year. And I didn't even realise what I was doing to myself. I wasn't dating so I had no one to look good for.

One day I asked my mum, who did my washing for me, why she had shrunk one of my dresses.

'I've just paid £60 for it and you have shrunk it,' I said to her.

'No Gemma, you are getting bigger, you're not realising it but you are really putting on a lot of weight,' she told me. I'm glad she did. I needed people to be honest with me. I tried to curb what I was eating and went through a period of fad dieting. I have done them all over the years. The Cambridge Diet, the Dukan Diet, the Cabbage Soup Diet, the Kate Moss diet (cigarettes and Diet Coke). But I didn't exercise and once the weight was on it stuck. I found it hard to resist temptation and I craved the comfort I found in food.

I believe the pattern for my comfort-eating was set even before I was born. When Mum was a girl she grew up poor and had nothing. Her biggest treats were food and when she had me she showed her love by giving me treats too. Growing up, my favourite times were going to restaurants with Mum and Dad, and on our weekend trips to London Mum might not have had much money but she would always treat me to an ice cream or a hot chocolate. Everything was focussed on the comfort of food, the way it was a treat, the way that even if you couldn't afford posh clothes and expensive bags and shoes you could treat yourself to a little luxury in the shape of a bar of chocolate. Mum made it better with food. She never said go for a run or get down the gym, it was always about having something nice to eat.

So I ate to make myself feel better. Often that did not work, though. I tried hard to stay positive but would often have dark thoughts. One night I remember driving over Gallows Corner, a large road interchange near my house. I was on the elevated section and the streets of Essex were spread out below. There must have been a song on the radio that reminded me of Robert because I was crying. I was hit by the dreaded feeling of anxiety that stalked me most days and a thought started to formulate in my mind. I could end it. I could drive through the barrier and end everything. It was just a flash in my mind. I didn't dwell on it but I considered killing myself for a split second.

I still felt I had no real answers about why Robert had left me and no matter how much distance I tried to put between us, I still wanted to know. It was driving me crazy. I used to get up and drive to work and as I was driving I had anxiety attacks, which felt like 1000 horses were running over my chest. I was breaking inside, I was so sad and hurt and confused.

One day at work I was having a chat with one of my colleagues, Joanna. We were talking about relationships.

'It is really rare that someone leaves a partner and nobody else is involved,' she said.

It had always been my suspicion that Robert had met someone else. I wanted him to tell me the truth and that conversation set me thinking. Had I been naive? Or just plain paranoid?

That lunchtime I got in my car and I drove to the barn. It was the first time I had been back and my heart was pounding on the way. I drove past to check his car wasn't there. I walked up the drive on shaky legs but I knew if he came out I would just have to front it up and pretend I wanted to see him. I didn't really know why I was there. I think I wanted to look to see if there was any evidence of a new girl staying in the house. I knocked. No one answered. I looked in the windows. I couldn't see any evidence. Then I noticed the corner of a letter sticking out of the letterbox. It hadn't been pushed all the way through. I pulled it back out. It was an Orange phone bill addressed to Robert. I pocketed it and went back to the car and drove off. At work when no one was looking I steamed the envelope open in the kitchen. I studied the list of numbers Robert had been calling and there were two numbers that kept coming up. One was a mobile, one was a London-based landline.

I rang the mobile. I felt strangely calm. For the first time in ages I felt in control of the situation.

A girl answered the phone.

'Hello, is that Lisa?' I asked, plucking a random name from my head.

'No, it's Hannah,' she replied. I hung up. I called the landline.

A woman answered and gave a company name. I quickly scribbled it down.

'Hi, is Hannah there?' I asked. I was put through to another extension and the girl who had answered the mobile number moments before came on the line. I hung up. Bingo! I felt good about my snooping.

I searched online to find where in London the landline dial code was and then Googled the name of the company and the location. To my surprise it was a women's clothing boutique. I was almost certain I now had the answer. Robert was seeing a girl called Hannah.

A few days later my friend Steph called me to tell me she had seen a girl get in Robert's car with him. By then I was certain I had found the truth and that the girl was Hannah. Anger flashed through me. I wanted to go round to the house and confront them both. I was hurt. I had no way of knowing whether Robert had met this girl when he was with me – perhaps he met her after we split – but Hannah had my boyfriend. I still saw him as mine.

I hadn't contacted him for over a month but in my anger I dialled his number.

He answered.

'How is Hannah?' I spat. 'Is she in our kitchen? Is she making herself at home in our house?'

I hung up. I was shaking. My mind started running away with me. I knew there was a window in the utility room of the barn that was always left unlocked. I knew how to get into it. I could creep in while they were sleeping and confront them. I let the anger wash over me and I pulled myself together. I felt betrayed, I felt let down but I accepted he was with someone else and I knew it was time to get on with my life. I told myself he was a lost cause and I never hassled Robert and Hannah again until a fateful day in November. It is a day I will never forget, nor will Robert I suspect.

I had decided I was going to throw myself into work and forge a career in sales. I used to sit on reception and watch the salesmen sell cars and think 'You ain't got it, you need someone with person-ality selling those cars'. I wanted to be a car sales executive. I wanted to be a success. My career had practically been put on hold but I could do more than reception work and admin. I had the eye of the tiger!

So I started doing extra shifts at BMW to show the manage-ment how dedicated and willing I was. I started taking on weekend shifts, particularly Sundays as I thought while I was there and it was quiet I could start asking the salespeople for tips and advice. I began to observe and question and learn the tricks of the trade.

It was after one of these Sunday shifts that I called Hazel and asked if she fancied going for a roast at a local carvery. She jumped at the chance and arranged to pick me up at 4 p.m. and take me to the Artichoke in Brentwood, which is a well-known pub in Essex that does a roaring trade on a Sunday. Its roast dinners are legendary and Robert and I had spent many Sunday afternoons there before I learned to cook a leg of lamb myself.

By the time Hazel picked me up I was starving and couldn't wait to tuck in to roast beef with all the trimmings. I was so famished I didn't even think about the possibility that Robert might have been in the pub. But when we pulled up in the car park my heart started racing. His car was parked right at the front.

Adrenaline started rushing through me and my mouth went dry. I was in shock. My heart was pounding in my chest and I went white. For so many months I had managed to put him out of my mind and now I was literally yards from him.

Hazel saw the look on my face.

'What's wrong?' She frowned.

'It's Robert, his car is here, he must be inside.'

'Right, we'll go somewhere else.' Hazel was adamant.

'No,' I said defiantly. 'Bless him, he's got no one cooking him his Sunday dinner like I used to and he's had to come to the carvery.' I must have been deluded.

I got out the car and couldn't wait to get inside to see him. We went to the front desk where we were informed there was a

45-minute wait. I wasn't listening. I was craning my neck looking through the sprawling pub trying to spot Robert. For once I was not thinking about food.

Hazel began to suggest that perhaps as the wait was so long we should go somewhere else, but I when she turned round I was no longer by her side. I was like a woman possessed. I went steaming through the restaurant looking for him. I don't know what was going through my mind. I was desperate to see him, in the vain hope that he would be on his own and things hadn't worked out between him and Hannah, but I was also full of anger and resentment.

I rounded a corner and there he was, totally unaware that I was there. I stopped and ducked round a corner. He wasn't on his own. He was with Hannah. The pair of them looked all cosy and were eating their Sunday dinners. I stared at him. I checked over every detail of him. He was wearing a pale blue shirt and had the white shorts on that he had worn the day he chased me through the fields to retrieve his phone. It was November so I assumed he'd been at the gym. They were facing each other, making conversation. I stood there watching for ten minutes. All the time a thought kept going through my mind. That's not my Robert. He looks different. He was acting differently.

As I watched from my secret vantage point I let anger bubble up inside me. And then it boiled over. I stomped over to their table. I had kept my mouth shut for over three months. I had buried my feelings and not told anyone how I truly felt. It was time to let rip!

I slammed my fists down on the table. Their plates jumped in the air and gravy spilled over.

'What the fuck is going on here?' I screamed.

Robert jumped. At first he was startled. Then he did the worst thing he could have done. He seemed to look at me like he didn't even know me.

That killed me. After all the time we had spent together and all the memories we shared it looked to me that he didn't even have the decency to acknowledge me. I started shouting obscenities; my anger was directed at both of them.

Hannah took the abuse. She sat there calmly then looked at Robert and asked if he could get me to leave.

By this time I was in tears. The whole restaurant was quiet. Everyone had stopped eating except for Robert and Hannah who it seemed to me were trying to act as if I wasn't there. I turned and left just as Hazel came to pull me away.

Outside I walked round to the side of the building where they were sitting and started banging on the window. I was smacking on the glass screaming.

'Oi, all of you in there eating your dinners. That girl has my boyfriend.'

Hazel had to restrain me and drag me away.

'You are going to get arrested and I'm not seeing you get locked up for him,' she said as she bundled me into the car.

I was banned from the Artichoke after that. If only Robert has said to Hannah 'I need to go and speak to Gemma, I owe her some answers,' I would have been able to control my feelings. But by not doing that he pushed my self-destruct button.

I was a wreck as we drove away. I was shaking and crying hysterically. Hazel, who was a great support to me, took me to Mum and

Dad's and told them what had happened. Mum made me a sweet cup of tea and Dad cuddled me until I calmed down. They were sad for me, they could feel my pain but my mum had a look on her face that said 'Get over it'. She knew I was destined for brilliant, greater things.

Robert contacted me the next day. He sent me an email and basically let me know that if I ever behaved like that again he would be contacting the police.

It wasn't that I wanted to hurt him. I wanted him back and I wanted the good times back.

But that episode was good in one respect. It made me realise that although my feelings for Robert were still raw wounds, I needed to get on with my life before I was dragged down. I worked even harder. I spent every weekend at the car showroom. And after a while I asked the manager, Lawrence Bennett, if I could become a trainee salesperson.

Lawrence was lovely and he had confidence in my abilities. He could see something in me and my efforts and extra hours had not gone unnoticed. He agreed to give me a trial. It was one of the proudest days of my life and a huge confidence boost.

Lawrence took me under his wing and taught me the finer points of being a sales executive. He encouraged me to hone my skills and my patter. I built up a huge amount of technical knowledge about the cars we were selling and after a while my trial period was over and I got the job. One of the perks was a company car. I'll never forget getting the keys to my first BMW.

The work itself felt very natural to me. I loved talking to people and would pounce on customers when they came in.

Lawrence used to give me pep talks and had a range of sayings and pearls of wisdom he would call on.

'If I fish for you Gemma you will never learn, you have to learn to fish for yourself and you will be able to survive,' he would say mysteriously, like a BMW Yoda. I was always hungry for the sale and although the basic wage wasn't much, I knew I could always top it up with bonuses because I knew how to get a sale.

In the first three weeks of the job I won sales executive of the month. I was on a roll.

Things were looking up until Christmas arrived. I had buried myself in my new job but when the showroom closed down for the holidays I was left facing the reality of my first Christmas without Robert and I was plunged into depression once more.

I started to comfort-eat, which was easy given the amount of food that was around the house at the time. I became increasingly anxious about Christmas Day. I reminisced about the family Christmases at the barn where I had played host and cooked for everyone.

When Christmas Day finally arrived I had worked myself up into such a state that I didn't want to see anyone or do anything. I tortured myself with thoughts about what Robert was doing. He would be there with her in my home.

I can safely say that Christmas was one of the worst of my life. Mum and Dad had made a huge effort and cooked a lovely lunch but I lied and told them I wasn't feeling well and that I needed to stay in bed. I stayed in my pyjamas all day and got the box set of *Sex And The City*. I lay in bed all day and watched every episode, crying periodically. I had bought myself a bottle of vanilla vodka and a friend had bought me a martini glass with lipstick and shoes engraved on it. I decided I was going to drink vodka out of the glass on my own. I shut my bedroom door and wallowed in my own self-pity. I was the Scrooge. I didn't go out.

A week later I went to bed on New Year's Eve. I didn't want to celebrate and I didn't want to hear the chimes at midnight. January came and went, I didn't celebrate my birthday, I wasn't interested. The only thing that I focussed on was work. It was my salvation and it kept me sane. I felt confident and in control when I was there.

I could gradually feel myself healing. I thought less and less about Robert. The grief and anger I felt in the months after we split were gradually beginning to subside. Some days the feelings would come back, however. Easter was hard because it was the anniversary of my pregnancy and the beginning of our end. I comforted myself by gorging on chocolates and sweets. Basically I found solace in food. It made me feel better but I had started to pay the price. I was getting bigger and bigger. I went up to a size 20. I had never been that size before but I couldn't stop gorging. Sometimes treats were the only thing in my life that made me feel better.

Then it was May, the month of his thirtieth birthday.

Even after almost a year, a part of me still wanted him back (another part of me hated him for what he'd done). I wanted him to know I was still thinking about him but after the escapade in the carvery I couldn't trust myself to knock on his door and say hello. I also knew I wouldn't be welcome. So I decided to write him a letter.

I sat down in my room one night after work with a pad and a pen and started writing. I felt like a lovesick teenager. At first I didn't know what to write. 'Happy 30th Robert,' I started. And then the words began to flow out of me. I reminded him about the times we had spent together. I tried to explain how I felt when we had broken up and I included news about my life, my new job and my family as he had been a part of it. I apologised about the carvery and tried to explain why I had behaved the way I had. I kept asking him why he had done what he had done. Halfway through writing the letter I broke down in tears but I carried on because it was like therapy. I was pouring all the stubborn thoughts and feeling out onto the paper. I told him I loved him. When I finished it covered eight sheets of paper, front and back.

It had taken me hours and I wanted to be sure it struck the right tone so I went downstairs and asked Dad if I could read it to him. Poor Dad sat with me on the sofa while I sniffed through every word.

'Hopefully we can be friends because the saddest thing about all this is that me and you started off as mates, we were best mates, we did everything together and it is very sad that we are now in this position,' I finished.

Dad nodded. He could see I was still grieving and agreed that perhaps the letter would give some kind of closure. The next day I enclosed the letter in a birthday card and I went to Clintons and bought a little grey teddy bear holding a heart with the words 'miss you' written on it. I used to send him cards with grey bears on them. I boxed the bear and the card up and sent them in the post. Robert had the decency to send me an email. It was formal but he thanked me for my letter and birthday wishes and said he would talk to Hannah about us being friends.

It didn't matter to me, it wasn't the point. I needed to get everything off my chest and that letter allowed me to do so. After that my life began again.

CHAPTER FIFTEEN

GEMMA'S BACK

know now that I went through a year of depression. I hid it from everyone, even my family. Throughout that period I was going through the motions and putting on an act. To the outside world I was bubbly Gemma but inside I was empty. There were periods when I would switch off my phone for days and wouldn't want to speak to anyone. I couldn't see a way out. I considered going on anti-depressants but I kept telling myself I would over-come it and that's why I never sought medical help. Work had been my life. I hadn't had a holiday for a year and I wasn't going out as much as I used to. I worked and slept, that was it. I enjoyed the buzz my new job gave me and I was good at it. I could persuade even the most doubtful customer to put in an order for a new car. The job meant that every time a new registration was issued, the sales executives were handed the keys to a new car. It was a great perk and I felt great driving around Essex in a brand new Beamer.

At first it was a culture shock going from a receptionist's job with no responsibility to a sales executive's job with targets to hit each month, but I learned fast. The showroom was in a place called Harold Wood in Essex and attracted a variety of local characters. Car dealers would come in and see what trade-in vehicles were available. Some-times customers traded in their old cars when they bought new ones and some of those cars were too old to be resold on the forecourt, so they would have to be sold on to dealers who would try to butter up the sales team to get good deals. We sold some expensive motors so customers ranged from high rollers to Essex posers. I was the only female sales executive in the showroom and I'm not ashamed to say that I got more attention from the male customers than the boys did. At first they were a bit jel (that's Essex-speak for jealous), particularly when I started winning the sales executive of the month accolades. But I made really good friends with most of them.

One of the team, Adam Stott, became a close friend and he was really the only person I opened up to about my problems and the heartache after Robert. Adam had ginger hair and was always sharply dressed in a suit and tie. He was a great salesman too and I found him inspiring. He was two years younger than I was but more senior in the team and, like Lawrence, he could see I had potential. He really helped me in those early months. He would talk me through the processes of getting orders but he was also into sales techniques and motivational training. He used to take himself off on courses run by a guy called Anthony Robbins, who is an American self-help guru who holds seminars on subjects such as health and energy, overcoming fears, persuasive communication and enhancing relationships. The courses cost hundreds of pounds to attend and teach people to unlock their true potential. Adam was well caught up in all of it and he used to tell me I could be anything I wanted to be if I put my mind to it. Adam would often ask me about my love life.

'You found anyone yet Gemma?' he'd inquire.

'Not yet Adam, I'm still looking for my Mr Right.'

'So who would that be then?' he asked.

I described my perfect man.

'He has to be a geezer,' I laughed. 'A bit of a gangster but with a big heart and a soft side. Someone who can look after me and who will let me look after them. Basically I'm looking for Tony Soprano.'

I loved the mafia series *The Sopranos* and I had a huge crush on the main character, Tony Soprano.

Adam laughed. He knew how upset I was about the break-up and he kept joking that he would fix me up with one of his friends. Then, after a few weeks he came into the showroom excitedly and sprung a surprise on me.

'I've got this friend I reckon you should meet,' he said. 'I think you'll like him.'

I raised my eyebrows.

'Why would I like him?'

'Because he's a lovely guy, but a bit of a rough diamond. He's like Tony Soprano.'

I had to think hard. I had not been on any dates since I split from Robert and that had been twelve months ago. I missed male company, I missed romance and I missed sex. I knew I couldn't sit around and be a wallflower for ever. I had been thinking more and more about getting back into the dating game but I didn't know how. I had been dieting. I was determined to get in shape. I even went to the doctors and got diet pills called Reductil. They worked by making me feel full after eating just small meals and they had a positive effect. I went down to a curvy 16 from a size 20. I was confident about my body shape and I liked the way I looked and so I no hang ups about that. I just needed that extra push to get me back out there.

Adam was persuasive.

'Come on Gemma, what have you got to lose? If you never try you'll never know. It could be a positive experience.'

He was using the motivational techniques he'd studied on me. 'Go on then,' I agreed.

Adam's friend was a guy called Alex. Adam arranged for the three of us to go for a drink.

We met in a bar called Oliver's in Hornchurch. It was a typical Essex cocktail bar full of glammed-up girls with fake tans, talon nails and false lashes and buff blokes with designer stubble, tight shirts and bulging pecs.

When Alex came in I tried to act cool but there was an immediate attraction. He was very good-looking with swept-back, dark hair and was smartly dressed. He was just my type. Adam had chosen well. We had a few drinks and the conversation flowed. My initial apprehensions about being with a man after Robert soon disappeared and I found myself getting swept along by the excitement of possibility. The night flew by and at the end of it Alex offered to make sure I got home OK. We shared a cab and when he leaned in to kiss me goodnight I didn't flinch. We locked lips and snogged. It felt exciting and sexy. I felt feelings I had not had for a long time and I liked them. Alex took my number and we arranged to see each other again.

He called the next day and invited me round to his place for a meal that weekend. I accepted. I was surprised how easy it was to get swept along in another relationship. My confidence was flooding back and I felt like a real woman for the first time in over a year. I refreshed my wardrobe and started watching what I ate. I started to think about sex and the thought of it thrilled me. I had been unfulfilled for so long. I vowed that I would not let things get serious as quickly as they had with Robert; I wanted to learn from the mistakes of the past and I wanted to have some fun.

I saw Alex for a few months and we had sex. It was reaffirming being with a man after Robert. It felt right. I had taken a year away from men. I wasn't on the rebound. I was ready to move on. It wasn't serious with Alex, we didn't do romantic dates and big gestures, there were no thrills or spills. It was sex and fun. I felt confident about showing a man my bod. I liked to dress up and show my curves, I went on ASOS and ordered myself a little size 16 dress. I felt a million dollars in it. I felt like the old Gemma again. I was honest from the beginning and explained that I wasn't looking for a long-term partner. There was no pressure on either of us and I had a great time. Alex was naughty and dangerous. We used to do mad things together. I would go to his flat in Chelmsford and we would read tarot cards together. It was the sort of young, silly fun that I should have been having while I was with Robert. The funny thing was that I never really knew much about Alex; I never really got his full job description: he was a ducker and a diver.

Things fizzled out naturally between Alex and me but the fun and the sex reawakened my interest in men. I was in my late twenties and realised that it wasn't easy finding the right person in the nightclubs and bars of Essex. Most men were either not my type or already in relationships. I found it increasingly hard to meet people so I thought long and hard about it and eventually took the plunge and signed up to Match.com, the internet dating service. I was embarrassed about having to register with an online site at first. I'm not sure why, it just seemed a bit desperate, but my friends were all supportive. I told them I was moving with the times and that the internet was how people met each other and they agreed. The truth was that at a certain age, and especially in and around

London, it was hard to meet people because everyone was so busy. I was hooked on my job and worked a lot of weekends, so I couldn't always go out, and I didn't want to be the type of career woman who realises when she is forty that she's missed the boat and ends up alone with a couple of cats for company. I still had the dream of finding Mr Right and having children.

I found the internet experience very daunting but I persevered as I thought it was my only hope. I paid my £30 a month fee and carefully filled out my profile details. I agonised over what photo to include and then monitored my account in-box to see if anyone was interested in me.

It didn't take long before I had a message. It was from a guy called Robert – I wondered if that was a bad omen. We exchanged messages briefly and Robert emailed and said he wanted to meet me. He suggested we meet in Hanbury Manor Hotel, a luxury hotel and country club in neighbouring Hertfordshire. Although Robert seemed good-looking in his photo and came across well in his emails I thought it was a bit forward asking to meet in a hotel. What were his intentions? Was he hoping we would spend the night together? I was suspicious so I asked my friend Shona if she wanted to come as a chaperone. What if this guy spiked my drink? Shona was game for anything and willingly agreed.

We drove to the hotel to meet Robert. I had emailed beforehand to tell him a friend was accompanying me.

Robert's profile had described him as 6 foot, but he was much shorter in real life and while he looked like his picture, he was definitely an older version of it. He was also too flash for my liking. They say first impressions count and I had made my mind up about Robert within a few minutes of meeting him. It was going nowhere.

We went to the hotel restaurant and the three of us had dinner.

Robert told me his wife had died. I felt sorry for him but all the time I was thinking to myself, what are you doing here Gemma? When he told me he had his own private helicopter I knew he was full of crap and it was time to leave.

I made the excuse that I had to get up for work the next day early and said goodbye to him. He didn't ask if he could see me again. I wasn't bothered. It was obvious from my body language that I wasn't interested.

We had driven a long way to meet him and didn't want to waste the evening so we waited in the car park until we saw him drive off in his Nissan and then went back in the hotel, booked a room and had a boozy night of girlie fun.

It was a very naive period of my life. I was just exploring what life was about and trying to catch up on the things I had missed out on. I went on a few dates through Match.com but there were no fireworks.

Then one day I was sitting at my desk at work filling out an order form and waiting for the next customer when a larger-than-life character swaggered through the door and caught my eye. He had swept-back blond hair and I could tell just by looking at him that he would be a handful. He was looking round at the cars in the showroom and had an attractive girl with him.

I was suited and booted in a Roland Mouret-style dress and I could see the man look over at me and look me up and down appreciatively. I pretended not to notice. I'd been dieting, my cleavage was on display and I was feeling good about myself. I wasn't against flirting with the customers. I was doing a sales job, I was going to use whatever I had to get the deal.

I walked up to him and introduced myself.

'Hi, I'm Gemma Collins, sales executive, can I help you?'

'Well Gemma, I'm looking to invest in a new motor and I'm torn between a Range Rover or a new X5,' he said.

I went through the basic questions with him.

'Will you be needing finance?' I asked.

'No love,' he sniffed. 'I've got an offshore account I can plunder for the readies.'

He had so much front and patter that I instantly fell for him.

'Can I take one for a test drive?' he asked.

I grabbed the keys for the demo car. He introduced me to the girl he was with – she was his sister – and we got into the car.

I was trying hard with my sales spiel, telling him how the car suited him and what it was like in terms of performance. I asked him his name and he told me. I'll call him Mr Blagger. He didn't know that I fancied him, I found him very attractive and funny but ultimately I wanted the sale out of him. I wasn't thinking about a date, I was just enjoying having a laugh with him. I pushed him to try and close the sale but he was playing me.

'I can't decide,' he said, rubbing his chin. 'The new Range Rover is a very nice car. It's a tough call after just one test drive.

I had a plan.

'I'm sure you'd feel differently if you had a bit more time with the car, why not take it for the weekend?'

He liked that idea and I persuaded Lawrence to let him borrow the car until Monday. I took his driver's licence for the insurance and noticed that his date of birth meant he was only twenty-one. He looked much older.

The weekend came and went and on Monday Mr Blagger

returned the car. I was looking forward to seeing him again. There had been chemistry between us, I had a feeling about him and wanted to see where it would lead me.

'What did you think of the car then?' I asked when he came to hand the keys back.

'I'm in two minds,' he said.

I tried to find out what the sticking point was. Was it price? Performance?

'We can do a good deal for you,' I offered.

But he seemed anxious and explained that he was in a bit of a hurry to get to a meeting and that he would be in touch. I was disappointed when he left because I was sure given time I could get him to buy a car.

In the showroom we employed a finance specialist to sort out payment plans for customers. He had access to certain databases and could run a customer's details through a computer programme to see what kind of finance deal they would be eligible for. If Mr Blagger's sticking point was money, I decided to get our finance guy to run his details through the system and see what we could offer him. That way, when he returned, I would have a plan worked out for him.

When the details came back I realised why he was so keen to leave the showroom before we started talking about money. As they say in Essex, Mr Blagger didn't have a pot to piss in. He had no offshore accounts and he lived at home with his mum and dad.

The funny thing was, however, knowing he had the front to con me into a weekend car rental for free only made me like him more. I laughed out loud. I couldn't stop thinking about him for the rest of the morning because for the first time in a long time I had met someone who made me laugh hysterically and put a smile on my face.

He had been in such a rush to get out of the showroom that day that he had forgotten his driver's licence. It sat there in my desk drawer for a few days while I waited for him to realise and call me. A few days later I was out with the girls and we were talking about him. I explained that this larger-than-life character had come into the showroom and blagged a car for the weekend and that I thought he was hot.

I'd had a couple of glasses of vino and I was feeling brave.

'I'm going to text him,' I decided. I had his number from when he borrowed the car.

I punched out a message in my phone. 'Hi, just to let you know you left your DL with me'. The text had hardly been sent when my phone rang.

It was him.

'I just got a message from you, I don't recognise the number, who is this?' he asked.

I told him I was the girl from BMW.

His serious tone changed.

'Hello darling, how are you,' he said. We had a quick chat, I tried to see if he wanted to come in and talk more about buying a car. He made an excuse then asked me what I was doing the following night. I told him I didn't have any plans.

'I am taking you out on a date,' he stated. 'In fact I am cooking you breakfast!'

I loved his banter, he was hilarious.

'To be honest I am not going to make breakfast but I would love to go on a date with you,' I laughed.

CHAPTER SIXTEEN

ALONG FOR THE RIDE

CHAPTER SIXTEEN

ALONG FOR
THE RIDE

liked Mr Blagger a lot. I knew he was prone to exaggerate and lie but I could handle that. He seemed like a nice guy underneath all the bravado. I was a sucker for a big character and he certainly had a lot of character. So as I drove to pick him up for our date I found myself getting butterflies. I was really nervous. He had no car at the time; he gave me an excuse about not being able to decide whether to buy a Mercedes, a Range Rover or a BMW. He asked me to pick him up at his house in Chingford. I knew it was his mum's house but I didn't ask him about his living arrangements and he didn't mention it.

It didn't matter because he was like a male version of me. He was a bit chubby but very attractive. On our date I didn't want to look too over the top so I wore a nice pair of jeans and a top with a pink blazer. I was going for the casual but glam look. I went out in the day and I had my hair and make-up done.

My heart was racing when I knocked on the door. His mum answered. She was a character just like her son. She called him and he came bounding down the stairs.

'Hello darling,' he grinned. Outside he saw my new BMW 5 series and smiled.

'Can I drive?' he asked. I was smitten. I let him. He jumped in the car and whisked me to the O2 in London to see a film. We had a laugh in the cinema, I can't remember what the movie was but when it had finished he turned to me and said: 'You've passed the test, I'm taking you to my favourite Chinese.'

The next stop was a place called Changs, a restaurant in east London. It was where all the old East End characters went and I loved the place. I found Mr Blagger charming and fell for him over a plate of spring rolls and chicken satay.

For the first time since Robert I felt like I was ready to lower my guard and let someone in. I thought Mr Blagger was going to be a serious contender, not a fun fling like Alex. We started dating properly.

Over the following months I got to know his family. They were lovely. His mum was very protective of him so when it started to get serious between us she invited me to the family caravan for the weekend. By this stage in our relationship all pretence about offshore accounts and luxury cars had been conveniently dropped. He even borrowed £100 from me. He'd always make some excuse. I took the lies with a pinch of salt. I thought he was lying to impress me and at that point it seemed endearing. He did get a car eventually. It was a orange SEAT Leon. Despite all the front he really had a lot to learn when it came to the finer things in life. I tried to educate him. I took him to Harrods because I thought it would be really nice for him to experience proper luxury. But he seemed to find it quite intimidating.

He was more comfortable in the caravan site in Southend and as I had never been in a caravan before it was a novelty for me. We were only there for one night and went to the clubhouse for a few drinks. It was a good laugh and we were all a bit tipsy when we went back to the caravan. We sat round the dining-area table chatting and for some reason his mum asked me about my previous boyfriends. I explained that I had lived with a guy called Robert and told her about the house and the life we had together and the places we had been. I didn't have anything to hide but as the conversation went on I could feel Mr Blagger bristling. He made a couple of barbed comments and then went off to bed in a mood. The next day he wasn't his usual chirpy self. I knew it was because of the previous night's conversation.

'You have to understand that I am a bit older than you and that I have had a past with someone else,' I explained gently. There was six years difference between us. 'You are the first serious man I've been with since then and I think a lot of you.'

I hoped he understood.

But that night was a tipping point and over the following weeks I felt the relationship slipping out of my grasp. He would blow hot and cold. One day everything would be fine and he'd be full of charm and bravado, the next he'd be off with me and wouldn't call. His birthday came and went and I bought him a £70 Barbour jacket. We went out on the Saturday night and I gave it to him. The following day he told me he was going to spend some time with his family and that he would come round and see me in the evening.

I chilled out for the day and was looking forward to seeing him. At 7.30 he called and told me his granddad had phoned him and was feeling down so he was going to take him for a Chinese. I thought it was a little odd but I understood.

'Don't worry,' I said. 'Take your time.'

He said he wouldn't be long.

By eleven o'clock I smelled a rat. Surely he wasn't keeping his granddad out that late. What had they done, gone to a club? My parents were in bed and I was getting ready to go up when he knocked on the door.

He walked in as if nothing had happened.

'All right babe,' he chirped. 'Sorry, Granddad was really depressed.' I wasn't buying any of it. My bullshit detector was ringing! Mr Blagger said he was knackered, went upstairs and sprawled out on the bed. As he was dropping off to sleep I went downstairs and found the brown Barbour jacket I bought him, slipped my hand inside his pocket and found his phone. I switched it on and flicked open his text inbox.

The list of texts told a story of betrayal. There were several to and from a girl called Amanda and it was obvious that he had been out with her, and not his grandfather.

As I read through them I felt the familiar feeling of dejection. How could he do this to me? I always knew he was a bit of a bullshitter but I underneath it I thought he was genuine and had genuine feelings for me. I was crushed. Then I felt anger. How dare he treat me like that after I had just built myself up. I had been on a high, I was feeling positive and he wanted to strip that away from me. He wasn't going to get away with it and he certainly wasn't going to take advantage of me. He still owed me money. I hatched a plan and I took his phone apart, removed the SIM, put it back together and put it in the pocket of his coat. Then I went upstairs into the bedroom and I slapped him across the face.

'Get out of this house you lying bastard,' I hissed.

He recoiled in shock.

'What did you do that for?' he said, cowering on the bed.

'I've seen the texts, I know where you've been.'

He knew the game was up. His shoulders dropped and he couldn't look me in the eye. He sloped off with his tail between his legs. I followed him downstairs to make sure he left and opened the front door and waited for him. As he slunk past I grabbed the back of his jacket. He flinched as I pulled it off.

'You can take this off,' I ordered. 'I paid for it with money I worked hard to earn, you don't deserve it.'

He didn't argue. I shut the door after he left. I didn't want him to see the tears in my eyes. I didn't want to give him the satisfaction.

I was devastated. Being cheated on felt like being stabbed in the heart. It bought back all the feelings I had after I split from Robert. History was repeating itself.

The following day his mum called to ask me for her son's SIM card back. He didn't have the guts to call me himself. I told her he would get it back when I got my money back and that evening they drove back to my house. We hardly said a word as we made the exchange. That was the end of Mr Blagger in my life.

I showed a brave face to the world but inside I was distraught. Another man, another failed relationship. I wondered what was wrong with me. All my friends were settling down and getting married. I was nearing my thirtieth birthday and was still no nearer finding my dream man. After Mr Blagger I went for a long period where I didn't want to get involved with men. Once again I found comfort in food and my weight went up to a size 18 and then a size 20, where it hovered.

During that period I turned to psychics to try and find answers and guidance. I'd see a couple of regular ones every month or so and have probably spent around £1000 in all over the years. I got great comfort from them and also advice about life and the path I was taking through it. I was never visited by dead relatives and nothing spooky ever happened but I talked through my problems with them and they used their intuition and openness to the spirit world to offer advice.

Another Christmas came and went and I found myself on my own. I was very depressed. There were periods when I would shut myself away and switch off my phone and wouldn't want to talk to anyone. All I managed to do was go to work. It took all my willpower, strength and motivation to get up in the morning and put on my make-up. I put on my armour, went to work and did the razzle-dazzle. I was Gemma Collins, sales executive extraordinaire, but in truth I really just wanted to lie under my desk and die. Those months taught me resilience. I had to toughen up in that time because I was working in a sales environment. I couldn't let people see my weaknesses.

It took a long time before I was ready to entertain the idea of being with a man again but there was no way I was going to give up on my idea of settling down with Mr Right. My friends joked that my life was turning into a quest to find him. I knew there was no point wallowing in heartache and so, when I met Mr Large, I found his charm irresistible.

He started chatting me up one night when I was out. He was another rough diamond and older than me; a bit of a wheeler-dealer and looked like he knew how to handle himself.

He asked if I wanted to go out for a meal with him and I couldn't resist his charm. Over the following weeks we would meet regularly.

It was a passionate relationship. He gave me the best sex of my life (you can work out why I call him Mr Large) and I loved being with him. I felt safe and protected. He was just the type of man I was looking for and in my heart of hearts I prayed we would be together.

'We'll be living together in our own place before you know it,' he would promise.

He bought me a diamond necklace. We talked about children. He didn't have any but would like to one day. He treated me like a princess, there was nothing he wouldn't do for me. Life with Mr Large was exciting. We went to casinos together, and stayed in hotels, it was fun and exciting. But it was a wild affair and although I loved him, I was living a fantasy.

'Hold on in there, I will be with you,' he would say, but the words began to ring hollow as the months passed.

I met him in May and in August Vicky was getting married. Mr Large was going to be my guest at the wedding. I was looking forward to it. On the day before the wedding a bunch of roses arrived on my desk with a note.

At first I was thrilled. Flowers in an office always cause a stir. I ripped open the envelope and pulled out the handwritten note. I recognised Mr Large's handwriting immediately and smiled.

Then I read the first line.

'I'm so sorry ...' Instinct told me what was coming next. My heart sank.

'What does it say?' one of my colleagues asked excitedly.

Then she saw my face and walked off quickly.

I read on.

I am so confused at the minute, I am going away, you are the only person I want to be with but I don't know whether I can ...

Tears blurred my vision. I had been fooling myself. I had fallen for the wrong man yet again.

The following day I went to the wedding on my own. It was a beautiful day and a lovely venue. I put on a brave face and almost got through the day without tears but as the vows were exchanged I couldn't help feeling that I had been cheated out of my chance to find happiness again. I had to do a reading in the service. It was all about love and finding the right person. I broke down as I was reading. Everyone thought it was because I was swept up in the romance of the day. But I was crying for Mr Large and our broken dream. As I walked into the venue there was a notice by the front door giving details of other couples who were celebrating their weddings that day. In a bitter irony, one of those couples shared the same names as me and Mr Large. It should have been us, I thought sadly.

I never heard from Mr Large again. He was a bit of a wanderer so who knows where he went, but meeting him was another life lesson. I was learning to toughen up and look after number one.

Amy Childs as Jessica Rabbit and me as a Bunny Girl at Harry Derbidge's birthday bash.

Me and Arg pop round to see my mum Joan.

Arg serenading me to 'Somewhere' from West Side Story.

A promo shot for TOWIE Series 4. I won't tell you what I'm thinking!

The new Posh & Becks out with Joey Essex and Sam Faiers.

Me, Joey, Sam and Cara Kilbey at the Television and Radio Industries Club awards.

ITV/Rex Features

Richard Young/Rex Features

Me and my bestie Bobby Cole Norris at Essex Fashion Week.

At Swarovski Crystallized Lounge with Lydia Bright and Lizzie Cundy.

Hanging out with the Wright Family (L-R: Nanny Pat, Carol, me and Jessica).

Amy and me at the Clothes Show Live.

A cheeky kiss with Russell Kane down Sugar Hut.

Rex Features

Alan Chapman/Rex Features

Me and Meg Mathews at Morton's Club in Mayfair.

Mwah! Getting papped after the TV Choice Awards.

TVChoice AWARDS 2012 In association with Daz

Nikos Vinieratos/Rex Features

Hiding my pain behind a smile at the National TV Awards.

Limbering up in support of Cancer Research UK's Shine night-time marathon.

Dan Kennedy/Rex Features

Surprise! Launching my very own clothes line The Gemma Collins Collection.

UK Press/Getty Images

Apple or cake? I know which one I prefer.

Gareth Cattermole/Getty Images

On *Loose Women*.
I love those ladies!

Talking about ill-fitting bras on
my regular slot on *This Morning*.
Keep those puppies under control!

Showing off my Christmas puddings dressed as saucepot Nigella Lawson for a photoshoot.

Laid bare. I'm happy to be me whatever size or shape I am.

© Can Management Ltd.

Stephen

CHAPTER SEVENTEEN

A BLAST FROM THE PAST

Most of my life I had two dreams; to be famous and to marry and have children. At the ripe old age of twenty-nine I found myself single, living at home with my mum and dad, a size 20, childless and working six days a week in a BMW showroom, with a string of failed relationships behind me. It's safe to say that things hadn't quite gone to plan.

But I wasn't upset or depressed. I was comfortable with myself. Sure I would have liked to have met a man by that point in my life but whenever the hard knocks came, which they always did, I always managed to pick myself up, dust myself off and get back on the horse. I was lucky. I had loads of loving friends and a wonderful family; nothing else mattered.

I didn't dwell on my failed relationships with Mr Blagger and Mr Large for long. Heartache never gets any easier but after you experience it several times in quick succession you gain the ability to move on from it quickly. I got upset, I ate more than I should have, I cried a bit, I wiped away the tears and I moved on. It was a process I had become adept at and I faced each hurdle a with typical Essex mix of stoicism and optimism. I knew my prince was out there and I knew my life would not always be the way it was.

I can't recall what I was thinking the day Ben called, after nine years apart, but I like to think I was spinning around on my leather chair in BMW optimistically planning what my life would hold in the future. The phone trilled and as my colleague Adam had explained when I started the job as a sales executive, every call is an opportunity.

I answered in my best clipped BMW-trained voice.

'Hello BMW Harold Wood, this is Gemma on the sales team, how can I help you?'

'Gemma, it's Ben,' came the rough reply on the other end of the line.

'Ben?' I frowned.

'All right bird, how are you?' he laughed.

'Where have you been?' I answered.

I knew where Ben had been but I didn't like to let on. I had heard on the grapevine that things hadn't turned out well for him. The problems begun after I last saw him many years ago. Soon after we drifted apart Ben had split from Leah.

On the phone Ben told me what he'd been up to over the years. I was happy to hear his voice. Every so often I'd thought about him and wondered how he was. A short while before he called I was with Mum driving and we'd passed his house. I wondered then where he was and what was going on in his life.

'What are you doing tomorrow, I hear you are single?' he asked. He'd obviously been doing his homework.

'I might be,' I laughed.

'You and me, King Will, we're going for a drink,' he said. The King William is a well-known pub in Chigwell where the in-crowd hung out. There was no negotiation, Ben wasn't taking no for an answer. I loved that he still had the confidence he had always possessed.

'OK Ben, see you tomorrow,' I said.

I hung the phone up with mixed feelings. It was lovely to hear from him again but it had been many years since we last saw each other. Ben had been through a lot and I guessed the experiences he'd had would have changed him. I was a changed person too. Not least in appearance. The last time he saw me I was in my early twenties and a size 10.

I never thought that I was going to enter into a relationship with him. I believed we were meeting as friends to catch up on old times.

The night before I met up with Ben I went out with Cassie and I stayed at her house. We'd had a few drinks and nerves were beginning to get the better of me.

'I really don't fancy this,' I confided. 'I don't know if it's the right thing to do. It's been a long time. Sometimes it's better to leave things as they were.'

Cassie was the voice of reason.

'You're jumping the gun a bit. He's an old friend, nothing more. Just go and see what happens.'

'You're right,' I agreed. 'I've got nothing to lose.'

But my instincts were telling me it was something else. Ben was flirting on the phone and I had been about five months single. I was missing men and I was open to suggestion.

The following night I agonised over getting ready. I tried on several outfits and in the end I wore all black to try and look slimmer.

I had butterflies in my tummy as I was driving to the pub. I was excited but nervous and kept telling myself it was no big deal.

When I walked in he was there at the bar, larger than life and full of the old Ben charm.

'Fuck me, who's stuck a pump up your arse and inflated you?' he bellowed.

I laughed. It was typical Ben. He meant nothing by it and he could always get away with it. He was so offensive that you had to laugh.

The years hadn't been very kind to him and he'd put on a lot of weight too, around four stone. But underneath it all he still had a sparkle in his eye. He'd made an effort. He'd gelled his hair and wore a pink shirt. The attraction was still there. He'd grown from a boy to a man.

We kissed as friends and looked at each other. Ben ordered me a glass of wine and we sat down for a chat. After a few minutes of small talk he opened up about his life since we last met. We were soon reminiscing about the old times.

Ben kept flirting.

'You're a good-looking sort, you are,' he said.

After a while he asked if I was hungry. Knowing the Ben of old I expected a grand gesture. I assumed he would want to go to a decent restaurant. I was wrong.

'Can we go to Burger King? I love the Chicken Royale with extra mayo,' he said.

'Not Windows on the World for cocktails then?' I joked.

We both laughed at the memory. It seemed like a lifetime ago when we had piled into the vintage Bentley. We'd both been through a lot since those days.

'We had some fun didn't we?' said Ben wistfully.

I nodded in agreement, lost in my own thoughts. We looked at each other and smiled. Something passed between us, a spark of recognition. We knew we had both aged and that we weren't those young carefree people anymore. Life hadn't turned out as planned for either of us.

Ben took my hand and we left the pub, got in my car and drove to Burger King.

Part of me wanted him to be the Ben he was back in the day, with the bling and the flash trappings. But basically, life had worn the gloss off him. I could see it in his eyes. That cockiness was still there, bubbling under the surface, but it was diluted and sometimes he'd go quiet and get a faraway look on his face.

After our burgers I drove him home. He lived on a nice enough street but, because he was a builder, his house was luxurious inside. It was cosy and Ben invited me in. I accepted.

I liked the new Ben. He was more considerate; he was still cocky but there was a vulnerability to him too. He was a single guy, recently divorced, who'd had problems in his life but was trying to get on.

We sat on his sofa talking about the old days and laughing about the memories and time ran away with us. In the early hours of the morning Ben made a suggestion.

'It's too late to be driving back home now Gemma. Why don't you stay over for old times' sake?'

I knew nothing was going to happen and I trusted that he wouldn't try anything on so I agreed. There was no sex. In the morning Ben woke at 5 a.m. because he had to go to work early.

He roused me before he left.

'I had a great time last night Gemma,' he said. 'Are you free tonight? I'd like to see you again.'

I had no reservations at all. It felt right.

'Of course,' I said.

After that we became a regular item. It naturally developed into a boyfriend–girlfriend relationship. It felt like it was meant to be. We knew each other well and that gave us a head start. We didn't have to go through an awkward stage of getting to know each other. We had known each other for years. As our relationship developed a little part of me started to wonder whether Ben would be the one I was going to end up with.

A few months after we got together he deemed it was appropriate to introduce me to his son. It was lovely to see him again as he had only been a few years old when I had last seen him. We became close and I treated him the same way I treated my nephews. I'd take him on shopping trips to Lakeside and buy him little presents. Ben loved that and his ex, Leah, was happy because she knew me and knew she could trust me with her son.

I got together with Ben in November 2010. It was a comfortable relationship. He didn't sweep me off my feet and I wouldn't say I was head over heels in love but I loved being with him. My parents loved him to bits too, which was important to me, but they also had doubts about him being a long-term prospect for me.

'Ben ain't the one for you, Gemma,' Mum warned.

'Give him a chance,' I countered.

And Dad wasn't impressed by his bravado.

I was content though and as my thirtieth birthday approached I allowed myself the luxury of thinking that I might actually have found my soulmate.

CHAPTER EIGHTEEN

EVERYTHING CHANGES

People who live in Essex have always known that it is a special place. While a lot of the other Home Counties are plain and boring, Essex has always had something about it. It's known for over-the-top glamour, expensive houses and interesting residents. Essex men are often portrayed as flash gangsters and Essex women as bimbos. There are hundreds of Essex-girl jokes, such as: How does an Essex girl turn the light out after sex? She shuts the car door. Or how do you make an Essex girl's eyes sparkle? Shine a torch into her ear. There is a bit of truth in both these stereotypes, but there is a lot more to people from Essex than that. Essex people are hard-working and industrious. They can spot an opportunity a mile off and they don't shy away from taking risks if there's a profit to be made. They are prepared to take the rough with the smooth and they knuckle down when times are hard but enjoy life when times are good. They like the finer things in life and they like to look good. Essex girls love fake tan, fake lashes and fake boobs. They love designer labels – whether they are genuine or counterfeit.

This unique Essex glamour and the interesting characters in the county attracted film-makers in 2010. I heard about a show being filmed in and around the area where I lived. People from a TV production company had been speaking to many of the local characters and visiting the clubs and bars in the area to find people to take part. I had heard that Amy Childs and Harry Derbidge, two of my friends from Raphael school, had been picked to appear and when the show was first broadcast in November 2010, I tuned in out of curiosity and was hooked. I even signed up to get alerts about it on the internet. It was strange watching all the locations I knew from my day-to-day life. I didn't know the rest of the cast. I had seen Mark Wright out and about but had never spoken to him, but that didn't stop me getting hooked on tuning in to watch his will-they-won't-they relationship with Lauren Goodger. I identified with her because I had lived through a string of failed relationships as well.

The show created quite a buzz around town. I started to notice the stars of it appearing in my favourite magazines and in the newspapers. I was never envious, I was pleased for them. It was about time Essex was getting some recognition.

As 2010 turned into 2011, fame and TV shows were furthest from my mind. I hadn't given up on dreams of being famous, but I was almost thirty and I knew I wasn't going to be a singer or a dancer any more. Besides, I had a career, which was my main focus. I didn't watch *TOWIE* often but thought I'd love to be in that show.

In early January I was getting ready for the busiest time of the year at the showroom. Twice a year number plates are changed and this affects the value of a car when it is sold second-hand. People who are thinking of buying a car often do so as soon as the plates change because they like to drive around in a car that people know by the plate is brand new. In January we were coming up to our plate change so it was an extremely busy time of year with new orders rolling in.

It was a few weeks before my thirtieth birthday and I woke up ready for a full-on day at the showroom. I put on my 60-denier high-shine tights from Marks & Spencer and left my room to grab some breakfast.

The stairs in the house were wooden and each week Mum would polish them religiously. Usually I took care negotiating the last steps because for some reason they could be particularly slippery after a clean. That particular morning I must have been thinking of something else because as soon as my feet hit the steps they flew out from under me. My legs swung up in the air and I landed on my bum right on the edge of the bottom step. I felt a sickening crack as my full weight crashed down on the base of my spine. I screamed.

Waves of pain shot up my back from my coccyx, the small bit of bone at the bottom of the spine that reaches down between your bum cheeks. I managed to lean forward and steady myself on my hands and knees but the pain was immense. I didn't know whether I was going to be sick, scream, cry or poo myself, it was that bad. Mum was in bed and managed to sleep through the noise. I panicked because I knew I was injured badly but I also knew I had to get in to work. I tried to pull myself up using the banisters but I couldn't. I convinced myself that the pain would die down if I could straighten up and I started crawling on my hands and knees to the front door. Each movement sent fresh waves of pain to the base of my spine. The nerves down my legs felt as if they were on fire. At the front door I took several deep breaths and managed to pull myself up into a stooped crouch. I opened the door and hobbled down the drive to my car, but tears were rolling down my cheeks. I somehow managed to get into the driver's seat but it was agony because my weight was resting on the area where I was injured. I gunned the engine and with gritted teeth drove to the showroom. Each little bump made me wince.

I pulled up at work but I couldn't get out of the car. My back had seized up completely. I rang one of my colleagues, Don, and he came over and helped me out the car and to my desk. I could hardly sit on the chair because the pain was excruciating.

Lawrence heard the commotion and came out of his office to see what was going on. He could tell by the look of distress on my face that it was serious.

'I think you need to go to hospital,' he said, frowning.

I was taken to the local emergency walk-in centre and laid out on the table. I was in so much pain that a kindly nurse came and gave me some heavy-duty painkillers, which knocked me out. I fell asleep on the bed there for a couple of hours while I was waiting to be seen. I was on my own. I didn't want the hospital to call Mum as she would have panicked and, as was often the case when I went through drama in my life, I thought it would be easier to deal with it on my own. I didn't want to bother other people with my problems.

Eventually I was inspected by a doctor and taken for X-rays.

When the results came back it wasn't good news.

'What have you got planned for the next couple of weeks?' the doctor asked as she studied the X-rays.

'It's my thirtieth so I'm going for a boogie and to have a drink with my mates,' I replied.

'You are going nowhere, you have fractured your coccyx,' she said. 'No work for a couple of weeks, and no partying.'

I was sent home in a cab with bag load of Diclofenac and pain-killers. I crawled into bed feeling miserable. Even though I was dosed up, the pain was still excruciating and no matter what I did, I couldn't get comfortable. Mum and Dad fussed around me and were brilliant. Ben came and visited and asked what I wanted to do for my birthday.

I fancied going to a luxury country mansion hotel and spa called The Grove in Hertfordshire and told him.

'I'll book it,' he said. It was a beautiful place and I kissed him and thanked him. It gave me something to look forward to.

Gradually over the following days the sharp pain in my back subsided to a dull ache. I was still taking the tablets and one day I had a strange experience. I was sitting on the sofa looking out the window when I heard a voice in my ear.

'Your life is about to change for ever,' it whispered.

It was so clear it made me jump. I'm not sure whether it was the medication or my intuition but it left me feeling a little unnerved. I went cold; it was like someone was standing behind me, and as I looked out the window I felt that change was coming in my life but I didn't know what.

By the time my birthday arrived I was still off work but was back on my feet and able to walk around. Ben had been good to his word and booked a night at The Grove and I drove us there the day before I turned thirty. We had a lovely meal that night. Ben was on form and swanning round the posh hotel like he owned it. On the morning of my birthday we woke up and went down to breakfast. We were helping ourselves to the buffet when I looked across the dining room and noticed Carrie and David Grant, two of the judges from the BBC talent show *Fame Academy*.

I nudged Ben.

'Look, it's the people from the TV,' I whispered.

When we sat down, they sat on the table next to us. I tried not to look, I assumed they would want a quiet breakfast without hassle but Ben started chatting to them and before long had concocted one of his stories. He told them he had retired at twenty-five and that we'd just popped in for an overnight stay. It was highly embarrassing but I didn't mind as I was used to his baloney. I tucked into my sausage, egg and bacon, drank my tea and let him get on with it.

After breakfast we packed our bags and left. All the while there was something niggling me. We'd had a lovely night and I was thankful Ben had booked it but he'd not actually wished me happy birthday. It seemed strange.

As I drove us out of the hotel grounds down the long sweeping driveway my phone rang.

I answered.

'Hello, Gemma, it's Mica at Lime Pictures. We are the TV company that makes *The Only Way Is Essex*. We've been speaking to Julie Childs, Amy's mum, and she told us that you are a bit of a character and we want to meet you.'

I blinked, I didn't say anything. I looked over at Ben who was looking out the window. Then I cut the phone off.

I genuinely thought it was a wind-up. I was thirty, I had been depressed, I had no kids, I had a string of failed relationships, my boyfriend hadn't wished me happy birthday. Fairytales didn't happen to people like me.

The phone rang again.

'Gemma, sorry we got cut off, it's Mica, we've heard you are a bit of a character …'

I interrupted her; my heart was racing. I remembered the strange experience I'd had a few days before.

'Mica, I can't really talk at the moment, can I call you back in an hour?'

My instinct was telling me to check out the call properly but not to tell Ben. I could feel him looking at me and I didn't want to talk in front of him. He was meeting his son at Top Golf, a driving range and golf centre in Chigwell and I was meeting Mum for tea and cake. I dropped off Ben, then grabbed my phone and pressed last number redial.

Mica answered.

'Thanks for calling back Gemma,' she said. She sounded lovely. 'Tell me about yourself then?'

'Well, I've just rocked back from The Grove, where I was having breakfast with Carrie and David Grant.' It just tumbled out. All the old theatrical training kicked in automatically and I hammed up all the details about my life. I had Mica in stitches.

'We want to meet you tomorrow,' she said.

I was buzzing by the time I got home. I tried not to get excited because I didn't know if I could take the disappointment if nothing came of it but I couldn't help it.

'*TOWIE* has called me, they want to see me,' I told Mum.

She was overjoyed. Her dreams were suddenly coming true. She was more excited than I was.

'Gemma, I always told you that you were destined to be famous. This is your time.' I've never seen her grin so much. She was grinning like a dog we had once called Daz; a little Jack Russell that was always baring its teeth. That day Daz had been reincarnated in

Mum's face. I had tea and cake with her and then went to Ben's that night. I didn't tell him anything but hardly slept because my head was full of hope.

The meeting was in an office building in central London. I called my friend Louise and asked if she would come with me. I wanted to introduce her to the TV people as well. I was still off work because of my back so was lucky enough not to have to take time off or explain what was happening. It struck me that although the back injury had been agony, it was worth every bit of pain if it allowed me to meet with the people behind *TOWIE*.

I slapped on the bronzer and lashes and pulled on my black rabbit-fur coat and headed to London with Louise. When we got to the address we realised the Lime Pictures offices were on the seventh floor. Louise has a phobia of lifts so we used the stairs. My top lip was sweating and I was gasping for breath when we reached our destination. After a hastily applied slick of Chanel lippy, a dusting of bronzer and a spritz of perfume I buzzed the door, composed myself and walked in. My heart was pounding but it felt so right.

A man called Mike introduced himself.

'Mickey baby, I'm Gemma,' I said, kissing his cheek. I was turning the Essex charm up to ten!

Mike explained that he worked with Mica to find interesting characters in Essex for the show and that Julie Childs had told them I would be perfect. The pieces had all fallen into place. If I hadn't been bullied at school I wouldn't have moved to Raphael and met Amy and her mum. And if hadn't met them I wouldn't have been sitting in that office talking to Mike. Everything in life happens for a reason, good and bad.

We sat down in a comfortable office and Mica came in and introduced herself. They explained that they just wanted a general chat about my life and that they were going to film me.

They asked me a string of questions, what did I do, what face creams did I wear, had I got a boyfriend. It was really random stuff.

'What are your dreams?' Mike asked.

'To find the love of my life, have two kids and have a white Range Rover,' I answered.

They interviewed me for about an hour and a half and when they started asking me about my love life I decided I didn't want to tell them about Ben. Something told me we were not going anywhere and I had a suspicion he would be against me being in *TOWIE*.

They asked Louise to come in and filmed us together. They then went and got another man, Gyles, who was the show's executive producer.

He was very posh.

'Define your way of life and how you want it to be?' he asked.

'Gyles, I want a Clive Christian kitchen,' I answered.

'What's that?' he frowned.

'You don't know what Clive Christian is?' I gasped. 'Google it mate, the perfume is 400 quid.'

When it was over they said they would be in touch. They gave nothing away but I had a good feeling. I knew I had entertained them. As I left I had a peek at the guestbook on reception and noticed a name. Joey Essex. I assumed it was another hopeful called Joey from Essex. I didn't realise that it was *the* Joey Essex and that he'd been for a similar meeting that same day.

I felt proud of myself on the way home. I was on a high. I was starting to believe that maybe things were going to change.

I almost didn't want to believe that such an amazing opportunity had come my way, just in case it was snatched away from me. I turned to Louise in the car.

'I think my life is going to change, Lou,' I said. That afternoon we went to Harrods and sat on the seafood stall there and had celebratory champagne, oysters and salmon eggs with crème fraiche, chopped egg and onion.

I tried to be cautious.

'What will be, will be,' I said. 'I am not going to get my hopes up but I feel this is my fate.'

Over the next few days I got calls from the people at Lime Pictures asking me more questions. The longer it went on, the more excited I was getting. My mind was focussed and I began to reassess my life. It was humdrum. I was bored with Ben, he hadn't even wished me happy birthday, he took me for granted.

Mica called and said she wanted to meet me in Essex with Louise and her family and film us all together. The film crew arrived and Louise's mum Pat Morgan (one of Essex's finest) laid on a Marks & Spencer spread. No one comes to an Essex house without a spread being laid on. Before they came round we got our hair and make-up done. Mica and Mike came again with their cameras and started asking loads more questions. They stayed for several hours and left, again without giving anything away.

A week went by and I heard nothing. Then they called again and asked me what I was doing that day. I told them that I had a friend who was selling fake fur and was having a fake-fur party. They asked if they could come along and filmed it and during the evening they took the girls off individually and asked them about me.

Mike spoke to me.

'What we've noticed about you is that although you have plenty of bravado, underneath that there is vulnerability, and that is the side we like and want to tap into,' he explained.

They were building up a picture of me and my life. I think they wanted to be sure I would fit into the show and interact with the other people in it. They were also asking a lot about my taste in men.

It was around this time that I casually mentioned to Ben that I had been approached by the people who make *TOWIE*. I didn't go into any detail and I didn't tell him the full extent of the meetings I'd had. He was unenthusiastic. He wasn't a fan of the show so I told him no more.

A few days after the fur party I was asked to go back up to the Lime Pictures offices in London to meet *TOWIE's* executive producer at the time, a woman called Claire Farragher. By this time I was back working at BMW and it was becoming harder to field the phone calls and keep quiet about what was going on. I was leading a double life where I was on the verge of something exciting and wanted to tell the world but couldn't utter a word. The people at Lime Pictures had taken pains to impress upon me the need for secrecy. I felt like I was living in my own spy story.

I rearranged my days off with Lawrence and told him I needed the time to go for an emergency medical appointment.

'Everything OK?' he asked.

'It's ovary trouble,' I lied. He quickly carried on with what he had been doing. Basically, I'd learned over the years that male bosses never question when you tell them you need time off for 'lady things'.

By then I knew Claire was one of the head honchos at *TOWIE* and that if I was going to meet her I must have been some way along the selection process. I can't remember the drive to the office because I was so excited. I was on autopilot dreaming of how my life would change if I was asked to go on the show.

I was ushered into the office and sat down for a chat with Claire.

She explained that she'd spoken at length to Mica, Mike and Gyles and that she'd watched all the tapes of me that the team had been filming.

Claire asked me questions.

'What would you do if you were walking down the street and someone shouted abuse at you?'

'Nothing, I'd ignore them,' I answered.

'What about if someone writes something bad about you in a newspaper?' she continued.

'It wouldn't bother me. Today's news is tomorrow's fish and chip paper,' I said.

Claire nodded.

'You're here for the talk of doom,' she said.

My heart sank. Did that mean they didn't want me after all?

Claire looked at me.

'I have to make you aware that if you agree to what we are going to ask you, your life could change for ever,' she said. 'We need you to sign a piece of paper. We want you to be in the show.'

CHAPTER NINETEEN

TOWIE

People automatically assume that because you are in a television show you get loads of money. I can assure you that, in *TOWIE* at least, that's not the case. Claire explained that if I signed up for the show I would get expenses of £50 a day. We get more now but that was the fee then. There would be opportunities outside of that to earn money from interviews and photoshoots but there was no big wage. I was also asked to sign a document promising not to misbehave or bring the show into disrepute. I was told that I would be expected to cooperate with the programme makers, be punctual and behave on set. I would get a seven-week contract and had to make myself available for filming when asked. I would get twenty-four hours' notice when I was needed.

I was listening to her but it wasn't going in. It was so much to take in. It was the big chance I had always dreamed about.

I signed their document as I knew whole-heartedly that I wanted to do this.

I was light-headed when I left the offices. I knew my life was changing for good.

On the way home in the car I started to get the shakes. I had been running on adrenaline and reality was setting in. I started to have doubts. What about my job, what was I going to do for money, I was thirty, not a teenager. I had stability and a career. I didn't call anyone. I drove home chewing it over. I remembered a conversation I had with Dad many years before. He was trying to drum into me that I needed to have a stable job. Back then I had laughed at him.

'I am going to retire at thirty what are you worried about?' I told him.

There I was, on the brink of starting in a reality TV show, without a wage and with just a seven-week contract.

I got home and blurted out my news to Mum. She screamed.

'I knew it Gemma, this is just the start.' She hugged me.

When Dad came in and I told him the reaction was a little different!

'I've been offered a part on that television show, *The Only Way Is Essex*,' I told him.

He'd never watched it.

'How much are they paying?' he asked.

'It's not really about the money,' I said. He raised his eyebrows. 'I get expenses,' I offered.

I had a little bit of money in the bank, about £4000, and I told Dad that while I was filming I could live off that. He wanted to see the contract I'd signed.

'You are giving up a really good job to be on a television show that might not go anywhere,' he said.

'This is going somewhere for me, Dad. All my life has been leading to this. This is my chance,' I argued.

Mum chipped in.

'Al, come on, she is making the right move. It's her destiny.'

That evening we had dinner and when Dad went to bed I had a chat with Mum.

'Ignore your father,' she said. 'You have to go for it.'

I started to work out a plan. I would do the show but also work at BMW because I could work around the filming days. In car sales you get days off in the week because you have to work weekends. I would speak to Lawrence and see if, for the seven weeks I was filming, he would give me some flexibility when it came to time off. If I needed time that wasn't owed to me I would take it out of my holiday entitlement or request to take it unpaid. If it all went wrong and I had to leave BMW and *TOWIE* didn't work out I fancied a change anyway and told myself I'd get a market stall or go and work in car showroom in the West End of London.

I knew I should tell Ben and I called him that night. We hadn't seen much of each other over the preceding weeks and when I told him the news he was underwhelmed. I was rapidly going off him.

The next day I went in to work as normal. I needed to speak to Lawrence and I was nervous about telling him what had happened. I asked to speak to him in his office.

'You don't know this, but for the past seven weeks I have been in a process of being vetted for a reality show,' I began.

'What one?' he said.

'*TOWIE*,' I answered. 'I got through and I want to be in the show.'

He was shocked and I explained my plan to him.

'Gemma, I still have a business to run here and I need a sales team who are reliable,' he said.

I decided to pull on his heartstrings.

'What if it was your son and he came to you and said that his boss wouldn't give him the opportunity. How would you feel? All I'm asking is for a bit of flexibility for the next seven weeks until I know how things will pan out.'

He agreed reluctantly. I think he knew he might lose a good member of his team. I also asked him to keep it private and he was cool with that.

It was March by the time I got the call to film my first scenes. They were filming the second series of the show and, on a Sunday night, I got a text from the production team.

'Hi, we need you to be at a car company in Chelmsford at 12.30 on Monday, look glam' it read. I sent Lawrence a message to say I wouldn't be in the following day.

I didn't know exactly what I would be filming or who I was going to be filming with. That was how *TOWIE* worked. They found out all about you and the relationships in your life and they then put you in situations to fit those details. I was a car salesperson so I was going to a car showroom. I guessed I would be asked to sell someone a car. There were no scripts and no lines to learn. Sometimes the crew would guide you on which subjects to talk about to the other *TOWIE* cast members and they would place you in situations that you would have to react to; however, the show was structured to make sure that the reactions and emotions of the cast were completely genuine.

I wasn't nervous driving to the location the following day, I was excited. I felt that a new chapter in my life was beginning and I was going to take advantage of all the opportunities it had to offer. I wore a black dress and made sure I was fully made up. I wanted to dazzle the cameras.

When I pulled up the cameras had already been set up and I needed to wait in my car until I was called for filming. When the time came for my scene I was briefed. I was told to walk on to the forecourt where I would be greeted by someone who would be looking at a car. My brief was to sell them the car. I was charged up. I tried to remember all my acting training but the thing about *TOWIE* was that none of that was relevant. It was mainly spontaneous. There were no actors and when the cameras started rolling I got nervous. I walked on the lot and there was Kirk Norcross, a bloke I had watched many times on the television. I did my best to burst on to the screen larger than life but I still had to do the scene three times because I got tongue-tied. The girl with bags of confidence was actually bottling it.

The crew told me to relax and not to try too hard.

'Just sell him a car like you would in everyday life,' they advised.

The whole point of being on *TOWIE* is to be natural. So that's what I did. I gave him the same patter I'd give any other punter.

I got in the car and was asked to take him for a test drive. It was a surreal experience but after a while I forgot the cameras were there and concentrated on trying to make the sale, even though there was no sale to make.

I knew of Kirk before *TOWIE* although he wasn't in my social circle. I was always in Sugar Hut, the club his father Mick owns, but I would never have looked at him because he wasn't what I'd go for in a man. He was a nice-looking guy but Mick was more my type. The producers of the show knew this. I'd explained to them who my ideal man would be in our initial interviews and they obviously realised that Mick would be right up my street.

My first day of filming went by in a flash and after that the scenes I was called up for came in thick and fast. The following day I was told to go to the Sugar Hut and to dress as if I was going for a night out. Again, I had no idea what the scenario would be or who would be there.

I was greeted at the club by two very pretty blonde girls; Sam and Billie Faiers. I introduced myself and they were lovely. They chatted about what was going on and they did their best to make me comfortable. I couldn't have wished for a nicer couple of girls to make me feel welcome. I had wondered whether it would be easy to gel with the cast who had already been together for one series but there was no bitchiness. Kirk met me at the club and was lovely too. I felt a little like the new kid at school so it was reassuring to feel welcomed.

I walked in the room and I was asked to take a seat at the table. They were building up a storyline and I was the main part. When it was my turn to walk into the scene I strolled in as if I owned the place. Kirk introduced me to his dad, Mick.

'Gemma come and take a seat, this is my dad,' he said.

I eyed Mick up and down. I fancied him, I'm not going to lie, he was my sort of bloke; a proper geezer.

We chatted and I naturally became a bit flirty. I was also told that someone else would be involved in the scene but I wasn't told who. As I was talking to Mick, a beautiful girl walked in wearing a grey leopard-print outfit. She had bright red lips and massive boobs. It was Chloe Sims, who became a very good friend of mine. Like me, she was a new member of the cast and was finding her feet. The producer wanted me to look her up and down, which I did. I didn't realise it at the time but I think they were building up a love-triangle storyline between Mick, Chloe and me. But I had no beef with her at all. As far as I was concerned we were making a TV show and I did as I was asked.

A week went by and I was called to do filming every day. It became obvious that it would be very difficult to hold down my job at BMW as well as appear on *TOWIE*. Lawrence was doing his best to allow me to take the time off but I appreciated that he had a business to run and I guessed that at some point something would have to give.

I spoke to Mum about my concerns.

'I'm finding it really hard to juggle the two jobs,' I admitted. 'I know I've been given a massive opportunity and I'm worried I won't be able to concentrate and give it my best if I have to work at BMW as well.'

I went in for a meeting with Lawrence to see if we could work something out.

'What do you want me to do?' I asked him.

'I don't know if I can keep you on in this situation,' he said honestly. 'We want to keep you. You are a valued member of the team but I need that sales team to be here and working.'

I realised I had put him in a difficult situation and I felt bad so I offered to resign.

Lawrence refused. Instead he offered a compromise.

'Off you go for a few weeks and I'll keep your job open,' he said.

However, the more I thought about it, the more I realised that the best thing I could do was hand in my notice and leave. I couldn't give *TOWIE* my all if there was pressure on me to go back to work, and without the safety net of a guaranteed job I would have no option other than to be my best on screen.

When I told Dad I had left my job for good he was worried.

I tried to reassure him.

'You know I am a grafter, I will always go and get a job no matter what happens,' I said.

It was a sad day for me when I left BMW. I had a brilliant time there, I met some fantastic people. Lawrence had given me such an opportunity. It had been a chapter of my life after Robert and it helped me get over a difficult period. I went without a party, speeches or a fanfare.

And the one thing I realised I would really miss was a car. People in Essex knew me as the glamorous blonde BMW sales executive who always had a new car. When I left my job I had to hand the keys to my company car back.

'What am I going to do Dad?' I asked when I realised my predicament. 'I'm on a TV show all about glamour and being flash and I haven't got any wheels. I can't drive around in a banger and I can't get the bus.'

Dad was a hero and came to the rescue.

He had bought me my first car when I passed my test and once again he put his hand in his pocket and bailed me out. He bought me a new car. I couldn't believe it. It was his way of backing me.

One Saturday morning Mum, Dad and I went back to BMW and saw Lawrence. We got a deal on an ex-demonstrator car. It was a brand new 1 series convertible with a 60 plate. It had no miles on it. Dad put the deposit down. Lawrence was there and he was genuinely pleased for me; he could see I was happy and he was getting a car sale so everyone was a winner.

I promised to pay Mum and Dad with an IOU.

'Well, if your television career takes off and you do well it shouldn't be a problem,' said Dad.

I think the episode reminded Dad of the time he was thinking of setting up his own business. He needed support from his father back then and he remembered how his dad helped him and realised I needed the same kind of help.

By now I'd told everyone I was on the show. It was real. I was going to be on television. I'd hardly seen Ben and we had just drifted apart. It didn't bother me. When I did speak to him he could barely contain his dislike of my new career. I didn't need his attitude complicating my life at the moment.

I knew I had made the right decision and when I was told the date of the first show, which was a Sunday night in April, Hazel decided to throw a *TOWIE* party for me at her house. She put on a lovely spread. She had carrot cake from Costco, she'd done the works. She even got me pink glitter *TOWIE* balloons.

Before the show my friend Alana told me I would need to set up a Twitter account. I didn't know what one was.

'People will start Tweeting you after the show,' she explained. At that point I had no idea how much I'd be in the final edited show and how I would come across. I didn't know what the public reaction to me would be or even if there would be one.

The show started at 9 p.m. and by 8.45 I was a bag of nerves. I knocked back a couple of brandies to steady my nerves. The house was full and people were asking me questions. When will your bits be on? How long will you be in it for? I didn't know. We all sat down with bated breath. The theme tune started. My mouth was dry. Mum was in the room. She had Daz's grin fixed back on her face. Dad didn't come. He wasn't bothered about the show (since then he's only watched one episode and that was because his dog Marco was in it – I don't take it personally).

The first part came and went. We watched the ads. The second part came and went. I wasn't in either of them. I started to worry. What if I'd been cut out of it all together? Had I made a huge mistake? Was I about to be the laughing stock of Chigwell?

The third part came on and there I was larger than life on the plasma screen in Hazel's lounge. I was so relieved I nearly cried. A cheer went up in the room. It was surreal watching myself on the screen. It is hard to describe. My first thoughts were that my hair looked messy and my make-up needed retouching. It didn't look like me. I couldn't gauge whether I was coming across as a likeable character or a show-off. The scene with Kirk and me on the test drive came on and in surround sound I issued the immortal line: 'I'm feeling it, are you feeling it too baby?' The room erupted in laughter.

At the end of the show Alana showed me my Twitter page. I had about 2000 followers. The huge majority of them were positive. *Gemma we love you... Gemma you are hilarious.* But one caught my eye. I had to reread it to make sure I was seeing it properly. *Who's this fat, ugly munter on my TV screen?* I stopped momentarily. I was in shock. I wasn't prepared for it. But I was on such a high that the good outweighed that tiny bit of bad.

The rest of the night was a blur. I had a few drinks, Mum went home and I stayed at Hazel's. Her son TJ came in and we watched the show again together. He poured me a brandy.

'You've cracked it,' he smiled.

I hardly slept and the following morning I headed home exhausted and collapsed on to my own bed. I was just dropping off when the phone rang. It was Alana.

'Put on Radio 1, Scott Mills is talking about you on his show,' she said.

I switched the radio on and screamed. The DJ was replaying clips of everything I said on the show. He was laughing and said I was his favourite newbie. A while later Alana came round. I was in a daze. I couldn't take it all in.

I hadn't eaten since the previous night and even then I was so nervous I had hardly touched the spread. I was famished and I knew where I wanted to have my *TOWIE* celebratory lunch.

'Let's go to the Mandarin Palace in Hornchurch,' I suggested.

It was a weird choice for lunch but it felt like the right place to go. It was where me and Robert had finished and my life had unravelled. But that chapter was well and truly over. I was beginning a new chapter. I had achieved something massive and my dreams were coming true. I had been back to the restaurant several times since that day with Robert and each time I'd had a feeling of sad nostalgia. But this time I tucked into my dim sum with hope and optimism for the future. The food tasted much better when it wasn't tinged with bitterness.

Life settled into some kind of routine. The gap between filming an episode and it being broadcast was very short. The producers did that on purpose to keep the storylines fresh and to keep reactions to events genuine. I was doing more scenes that involved Mick, including the famous scene when I baked him an apple pie.

I cottoned on after the first show what was happening; that they were putting us together to see what would happen and whether a relationship would develop. I hoped it did because I genuinely had the hots for him and I wanted a date with him. I thought he liked me too. I dreamed I was Mick's bird. Ben was out of my life at this point and I could see a future with Mick. I wanted to be the woman who looked after him.

The seven weeks came and went in a flash but the moment that sealed it for me and for my place in the next series and in the public's heart was when Mick left me high and dry at the pool party. Everything had been leading to that point. If you haven't seen the episode I'll explain.

Throughout the series there was a will-they-won't-they story-line involving Mick, Chloe and me. There was a connection there between us and we had been placed in situations together that allowed for the possibility that something could happen. I was hoping Mick would ask me out.

On the last week of filming we were told to get our swimming costumes on because there was a pool party at a house in Ching-ford. During filming I was told to go to the bar with Maria Fowler and wasn't told what would happen next. The cameras started to roll and I looked round at Mick, then he started walking towards me with a bottle of champagne. He had been given it and he had to pick someone at the party to share it with. When I saw him swagger towards me I believed we were going to share a romantic drink in the sun. I was swept up in the romance of the situation. It was going to be the most wonderful moment of my life. I am a dreamer so I had concocted the idea of me and Mick in my head.

We only did three or four scenes together but I did my enquiries about him and I was told he was a nice chap. I had seen other relationships develop in the show that spilled out into real life and I thought it could happen for me and Mick. While he was working at the club I would be at home cooking him a nice dinner. All these thoughts were swimming around my head at the party when Mick walked straight past me and gave the bottle to Nicola Goodger, Lauren's sister.

I was surprised by my own reaction. I could feel the tears welling up in my eyes and although I tried to tell myself to stop being so silly, they started to roll down my cheeks. I couldn't keep my emotions in check. I stood there at the bar while a surprised Maria tried to comfort me.

It hurt that Mick walked past me, but I didn't cry because of him. Yes I fancied him, but if he didn't fancy me that was fair enough. Basically, the tears were for much deeper reasons. Mick's choice to give his bubbly to someone else represented rejection. I wasn't crying for him, I was crying because that moment brought back memories of all the other rejections that had gone before. I had been living in a bubble for several months. My confidence was sky-high but in that moment I was reminded of the vulnerabilities and insecurities that I kept buried deep down; those same qualities the producers had seen in me and had wanted to exploit. I didn't act; the tears were genuine.

In hindsight, I'm glad it all happened. Not only did that event teach me that Mick was not for me but it also let the public see the real side of me that I usually keep hidden. At heart I was just a girl who wanted to be loved.

CHAPTER TWENTY

BOOT CAMP

With the first series over, my place in the *TOWIE* cast was assured for the next series but while I waited for filming to begin I was faced with an eight-week break and a problem.

I needed to earn some money. Even if I hadn't given up my job at BMW, it would have been impossible to work there again. I was getting recognised on the street. The first time I was asked for an autograph I was filling my car with petrol when a girl at the pump next to me came bounding over.

'Oh my God, I love you on *TOWIE*,' she screamed.

I was embarrassed at first but I'd be lying if I said I wasn't pleased.

I had got to grips with Twitter and realised that I had a fan base. People were sending me hundreds of messages a day. They came from all sorts; from men making filthy suggestions to larger ladies who told me how refreshing it was to see someone like me on TV looking fab. I didn't consider myself famous. Even to this day I don't say I am famous. I say I am a TV personality.

I started to get offers from magazines and newspapers to do interviews and photoshoots and celebrity agents were also calling, asking if they could manage me. One of them sounded particularly switched on and genuine, a guy called Mark Thomas. I arranged to meet him in St John's Wood in London and I liked him straight away. He seemed honest and open. I signed up with him.

During the break in filming Ben got back in contact. We met up and we started seeing each other again. But he had a real problem with me being on the show. He hated it and said I should be doing something classier. He didn't say anything about the Mick situation but I guessed he was jealous.

I told him straight.

'Ben, this is the chance I have always been looking for. It's what I worked towards when I spent all those weekends in drama school. If you can't accept it then we might as well walk away from each other.'

Two weeks after signing with Mark, he called me with an offer. A magazine was offering me a lot of money to go to boot camp and lose some weight. It seemed like a good deal to me so I agreed, but it wasn't something I wanted to make a habit of.

In all honesty I was not bothered about my weight. I had reached the point in my life where I was what I was. I was happy with myself. People accepted that I wasn't stick-thin. My friends and family never mentioned it. It was only while I was doing the first series that I started to notice people in the media commenting on it. Initially I wasn't troubled. It probably affects me more now than it did then because I've since been subject to a few nasty weight-related headlines – one asked 'Whose tent did you borrow?' above a picture of me at an awards event.

That initial negative comment following my first appearance on *TOWIE* was the first of many. The nasty comments would appear under photos of me on websites and increasingly on Twitter. They were always targeted at my weight. At first, I tried to ignore them but as time went on they began to upset me more and more. I started taking it to heart. Clearly I have an issue with my weight so why did people feel the need to pick on me for it? They were internet trolls and I was an easy target. It was bullying. I wondered what type of person would feel the need to do that. They were sick and twisted individuals.

While I was waiting for details of the boot camp to be finalised I was offered money to do a naked shoot for *Heat* magazine. It was a paid shoot. I didn't have to think too hard about it. I said yes on the condition that it was tasteful and that they didn't show anything they shouldn't.

'It needs to be a positive piece that addresses the fact that I am not stick-thin but am curvy and proud,' I explained.

The photographs were done by a female photographer in a studio in London and I was allowed to see each shot to make sure I was happy with what was being taken. There was nothing seedy about it. I had an eye infection the day of the shoot so I didn't feel particularly sexy, but I was coaxed along by the photographer and it was a positive experience. It was actually a laugh. I did an interview to go with the photographs and I spoke about having a positive body image. I didn't go to McDonald's every day and eat junk food, I explained, and people should just accept that I wasn't stick-thin.

When the pictures were published they caused a stir but it was all positive. They were debated on Matthew Wright's show *The Wright Stuff* and presenter Anne Diamond said I was cherub-like.

Ben was less complimentary.

He called the day the mag was published. To say he was unhappy was an understatement.

'Listen Ben, this is me, this is what I am now. This isn't going anywhere,' I sighed. I'd had enough of his attitude and a few days later I left for boot camp without getting in touch.

I'd had to sign a strict contract. The magazine wanted me to slim from a size 20 to a 12. I would stay at the No1 Boot Camp in Norfolk for six weeks on a residential basis. I couldn't be photographed in that time and had instructions not to talk to journalists or to be seen out. It was a lot of weight to lose in a short time and I felt apprehensive about being away from home for so long. I arranged for Vicky to come with me for the first week. I knew I would need moral support.

When I left home to go to the camp I felt awful. It seemed like such a long time and I knew it would be hard. On the drive there I kept making excuses about why I should turn round. Vicky told me to pull myself together.

One of my issues was that I didn't particularly want to lose weight at that time but I needed the money. To console myself I stopped on the way and had a Twix. It was the last meal of a condemned person and I savoured every crumb.

No1 Boot Camp was in a very pretty setting, nestled in the countryside and woodland of Norfolk. The place itself was like a spa and was very comfortable, but I knew that underneath the luxury the regime was going to be hardcore. I'd never been interested in gyms or exercise so the whole set-up was alien to me.

I couldn't stop moaning.

Vicky gave me a pep talk.

'You've come here to be healthy and lose weight. This is the best place to do that. You have a brilliant opportunity. Give it a chance, you might actually enjoy yourself.'

I tried to be positive and nodded but inside I felt rubbish. My life was changing so rapidly: I was now living in a world where people were offering me money to do weird things like pose naked and go on diets and I hadn't had time to catch up and take it all in. I felt exposed and overwhelmed.

The first afternoon at boot camp we were met by a guy called Ricky who gave us an induction. I was put on the scales. I weighed 17 stone 11lbs. I got off the scales and was told the rules. Our food intake would be strictly controlled and every day would be full of exercise.

'And you can only drink herbal tea,' Ricky finished.

That was almost the last straw. I loved a cuppa. I felt like crying.

We got in our room and I looked at Vicky with big, sad, pleading eyes.

'Please, please can we go to the village and get a chow mein,' I begged. I had noticed a Chinese takeaway on the way in.

She gave me a mock slap around the face and told me to pull myself together.

The next morning I got my exercise gear on and went to start boot camp. And to my surprise, for two days I quite enjoyed it. But we were being eased in gently and by day three I was suffering headaches and exhaustion. I had real trouble with the discipline.

The days started at 7 a.m. with a three-mile run or jog before breakfast, which was a dollop of porridge. Then there were exercise classes. Snacks consisted of one carrot or one bit of cucumber and some hummus to dip it in. Lunch was soup or a small salad and then in the afternoon there was a four-hour walk. Dinner was steamed veg and chicken or fish.

Halfway into week one I staged a sit-in and sent Vicky to tell Ricky I wasn't well and needed to go home.

He came up to my room and told me I wasn't going anywhere and that everyone hits a difficult period in the first week.

I had my dad's voice in one ear and my conscience in the other reminding me that I had signed a contract and if I didn't see the process through I would not be getting any money.

I struggled through and by the end of the first week I felt I had got over the worst. I felt a sense of achievement and I did feel better about myself. At the weekend I took Vicky back and I had a sneaky curry while I was at home. I had the healthy option: tandoori king prawns with nan bread and the korma sauce on the side. I enjoyed every mouthful. Mum looked at me and said I didn't look any different.

In week two a new group of boot campers arrived and I did a double take at dinner when I looked up from watery bean soup and saw Meg Mathews sitting at the dining room table. OMG, I thought to myself. She caught me looking at her and she smiled and came over.

'Hello Gemma,' she said. I was shocked that Meg knew my name. I always liked her because she was quite out-there. We started chatting and she introduced me to the party of people she was with. They were a glamorous bunch and lots of fun. All of a sudden boot camp had become exciting.

The weather turned sunny and I started to loosen up and enjoy myself. In the evenings I used to sing Dolly Parton songs with one of the other boot campers. The week shot by and when Meg left we exchanged numbers.

I stayed at the boot camp for another two weeks and had lost quite a bit of weight by then. I started having a few breaks away and arranged to meet Meg. I met her in Primrose Hill, a posh enclave in London, and she asked me a favour.

'My daughter Anais loves *TOWIE*. Can you show her around Essex for a day please?'

I told her it would be an honour and a few days later Anais Gallagher, accompanied by a friend of Meg, arrived at Mum and Dad's three-bedroom semi for a tour of Essex. I took her to Minnie's Boutique. It is fun and all pink. Sam and Billie who run it are lovely too. Anyone who watches *TOWIE* wants to go there. I had a word with the local riding stables and took her horse riding. Then I took her to Nando's for dinner.

Back at boot camp the following week I got a call from Ben.

He was full of remorse.

Ben knew the right buttons to press with me. He could infuriate me to the point where I pushed him away but there was also a bond between us and I genuinely thought a lot of him. I just couldn't see a way forward with us if he carried on behaving the way he was when it came to my new life.

'Let's talk when I finish the boot camp,' I told him. We had a brief chat and I told him I was finding it hard going.

After the break I'd had, I found the fifth week particularly hard. I was exhausted all the time. Towards the end of the week my phone rang. Ben's number was displayed on the screen.

'Hello?' I answered.

'Do you know Lamsey Lane?' he asked.

It was the road the boot camp was on.

'Yes, why?' I questioned.

'Because I'm there now, can you come and pick me up?'

Shocked, I drove up the road to find Ben standing on the corner clutching a Tesco carrier bag that contained a toothbrush and a spare pair of pants.

He took one look at me and exclaimed: 'You look fucking starving. What's happened to my girl?'

He explained that he wanted to see me and that I had sounded miserable on the phone. He had persuaded a friend to drive him there. I couldn't leave him and part of me was glad to see a familiar face from home, so I took him back to my room.

He was worried about me.

'You need a steak,' he said.

He knew how to get round me and the idea of a fat juicy steak and chips did seem very appealing.

I convinced myself that having already lost two and a half stone I would be able to drop the rest in another week and that I needed the rest to be able to make the last push.

We snuck out like a couple of escaping prisoners and drove to a nearby country hotel where we booked a room. I went AWOL and turned off my phone because I knew it wouldn't be long before the boot camp told Mark and he would be calling.

In the hotel restaurant I tried to revive myself with steak, egg and chips washed down with Diet Coke. I barely spoke but I savoured every mouthful.

We went upstairs to our room and I had a bath. I put my nightie on and got into bed. Ben climbed in beside me. His hands started wandering. I batted them away. I was exhausted. I just wanted to sleep.

The next morning he was still seemed concerned about my lethargy and he rang a private doctor in Essex and arranged for me to have an appointment that day. He was trying very hard and kept telling me how much he loved me and how much he cared. I was gradually melting and it felt good to have someone to look after me because I felt awful. We had a full English breakfast and I drove us home. Later that day I saw a doctor who diagnosed me with anaemia, which explained the tiredness. Ben took me back to his house and looked after me. I have to admit it was a wonderful weekend with him and I started to see past the troubles we had been having.

We had a long discussion about the future.

'Look, if we are going to be together you have to accept that I am going to do this.' I was talking about *TOWIE*. 'I have been given a massive opportunity, you can either be part of it or not.'

Ben understood that my life had changed and agreed to try and accept what those changes meant. We sealed it with a romantic weekend together in his house. I kept my phone turned off and on Monday, having rested and taken iron tablets, I felt well enough to go back to boot camp for the final week. When it was over I was proud of myself. I had dropped to a size 14, the smallest I had been for many years. I still had to starve myself and keep hidden because the magazine needed to do a photoshoot to show off my new body along with the photos they had done before the boot camp. They would then run a big 'before and after' feature showing what a miraculous change I had made. That was the plan anyway.

On the day of the shoot I could sense grumblings from the staff. I was basically feeling ill because I hadn't eaten for twenty-four hours. They started to complain because I wasn't a size 12, which had been the original deal.

I couldn't believe what I was hearing. It was so deflating after all the hard work.

'Don't you understand what a feat it is to go from a size 20 to a 14?' I asked.

I felt crushed by the criticism. For me to drop three dress sizes in that amount of time was a huge achievement. I did the shoot and felt worthless afterwards. I wondered why I had bothered. The whole weight-loss-for-money thing seemed seedy now. I went home to Ben that night, had an Indian and enjoyed it.

A few days later Mark called with bad news. The magazine was withholding half the money because I didn't lose as much weight as my contract stipulated. I was livid and for the first time I started to question whether I really wanted to be involved in an industry that treated people the way I had been treated.

I vowed that in future I would be pickier about the type of work I did. The world would have to accept me for who I was, curves and all. I wasn't going to change for anyone. Meanwhile Ben and I repaired our relationship but that didn't last when I started back on *TOWIE* in August.

Charlie King and I were just work friends. But it was hard for Ben to see me getting to know other men in the show so publicly. I told the people at *TOWIE* I already had a man, they met him and there may even have been a chance for Ben to be on the show, but it wasn't something he wanted to get involved with.

As filming finished on my second series Mark, my agent, called with some good news. ITV2 had been in touch and they wanted me to fly out to Australia to be on *I'm A Celebrity Get Me Out Of Here NOW!* I screamed when I got the call. I'd always hoped that *TOWIE* would help build up my public profile and then I could eventually try some presenting jobs. I am forever indebted to *TOWIE* for what it has done for me but I did need to earn money so I wanted to try a few other things alongside it. I needed more stable income.

A go at presenting on a mainstream show was just what I needed on my CV. Ben was pleased too.

I flew to Australia first class and sat on the panel with host Laura Whitmore. I was unusually tired for the week I was there and put it down to jet lag. It didn't affect the time I had though. I loved every second. It was a dream come true. While I was there I saw Joe Swash and I made a very firm friend in the comedian Russell Kane. I was there to support Mark Wright from *TOWIE* I and started hanging around with his family, who were all lovely. Two days before I was due to fly home Pete Andre arrived and we did some filming together. It was the highlight of the trip. When I was growing up I loved Peter and meeting and working with him was amazing. He was filming for his show *Peter Andre: My Life* and asked me to be on it. We shared a car to the *I'm A Celeb* set in the jungle and he gave me some advice and told me that if I wanted to do more presenting work I should have a chat with his agent, Claire Powell.

When I got back I was still feeling washed out but put it down to the travelling. I told myself I would have to get used to it if I wanted to lead a jet-set lifestyle. It was November and for some reason I couldn't fathom, I started to get the urge to clean Ben's house where I was staying most of the time. The day after I arrived back I started cleaning and clearing all the cupboards. Ben and I still had disagreements and I was beginning to realise that he would never accept the new life I had. We blew hot and cold, our relationship was on and off all the time. We'd make up, then he'd do something and I would leave again. Underneath it all I wanted it to work out but I had so many doubts.

I spent Christmas Day at home with my parents and that was when the sickness started. Waves of nausea swept over me and although we had arranged to go out with my parents for Christmas lunch I had to go to bed instead. I knew then what the issue was. I had a feeling I was pregnant.

A few days later I did a test and my suspicions were confirmed. As the blue line appeared on the plastic stick my head was a jumble of hopes and doubts. Were Ben and I strong enough, would I still be able to work on *TOWIE* if I was expecting? Because of what had happened in the past I didn't know if I could go through with another termination. I was scared and confused. I didn't know what to do or where to turn for help and advice. I felt like I was trapped in a nightmare. I wanted the baby, I wanted children but I didn't know if Ben would. When I told him the news my suspicions were confirmed. His response was lukewarm, he sounded worried. But I had decided I wanted the baby no matter what and I didn't tell anyone, not even my mum and dad, because I wanted to give it three months to make sure everything was fine.

I had arranged to spend New Year's Eve with my parents. We were going to a posh country club hotel in Chelmsford called La Maison Talbooth. I had cooled things with Ben and wanted to get away to try and work things out in my head so I was shocked when he turned up. He'd paid the £150 taxi fare to come and talk.

He explained that he didn't think we were strong enough and was worried that a baby would make things worse.

'Let's call it off Ben,' I said sadly. I didn't believe we could make it work and I knew that Ben would never be happy as long as I was on *TOWIE*.

I made a resolution on New Year's Day that I would concentrate on my career while I was pregnant, so that after I had the baby I would be able to support us both. I started to think about finding another agent. My dream job was presenting a show such as *This Morning*. I arranged to meet with Peter Andre's manager Claire Powell and signed up to her company CAN. I was a big fan of what she had done for both Peter and Katie Price and she also represented my pal Amy Childs.

At the end of January I had the National Television Awards to look forward to. It would be the most prestigious event I had attended. Everyone who was anyone in show business would be there and I wanted to look knock-out.

The day before the ceremony I started to feel ill. My tummy was tender and the nausea returned. I accepted that it was all part of pregnancy and I ate some ginger biscuits to try and calm my stomach because I'd read that they helped. I was supposed to be trying on dresses for the event but the pain got worse and I had to rely on my friend, stylist Jeff Mehmet, to run around and source a dress for me. He found me a gorgeous Anoushka G vintage nude and black floor-length gown with beautiful lace and beaded detail.

I tried to sleep the sickness off but couldn't, and by midday I had started to get excruciating pains in my stomach. I was panicking. I didn't know what was happening but I feared for the baby. I prayed it was a stomach bug or food poisoning but the pain was becoming so acute I knew something serious was happening inside me.

I got out of bed and staggered to the landing to call Mum. I needed to go to a clinic. I started to feel the urge to push and the pain was coming in waves. Was I having contractions? I was terrified. I clutched the top of the banister for support. Then the bleeding started. I looked down in horror to see thick clots running down my thighs. I collapsed screaming.

Mum ran up the stairs, alerted by my screams, to find me rolling around in the floor in agony clutching my stomach. I was covered in blood. It was like a scene from a horror movie. She immediately called an ambulance. In the minutes it took to arrive I felt a sickening, tearing pain deep inside me, and then the pain started to subside. I was shaking and crying. I knew instinctively what had happened. I had lost my baby.

Thankfully I don't remember too much about what happened next. I was in shock. I was rushed to hospital where I underwent a scan, which confirmed what I already knew. I was padded to try and contain the bleeding and monitored. I was wheeled into a recovery room where I lay dazed, trying to make sense of what had happened.

All the while my phone was ringing and people were leaving messages to ask me what dress I was wearing to the NTAs. The feeling of loss and desolation ate away at me. I felt guilt. Was I being punished for having a termination all those years before? Would I be able to get pregnant again?

I was released later that evening and spent the night with Mum and Dad. I needed the security of home. I needed to be strong and brave.

The following night I went to the awards and I put on the sparkle. No one knew what I had been through. I got loads of compliments about my dress. No one knew that underneath it I was packed out with surgical padding because I was still bleeding. It should have been one of the best nights of my life but I look at those pictures now and all I can see is the pain and sadness etched on my face beneath the fake smiles.

CHAPTER TWENTY-ONE

ARGIE BARGIE

couldn't get Ben out of my mind. I'd been so used to our on/ off relationship that I didn't know any more where we stood with each other. He had a right to know about the miscarriage and I told him. He said he was sorry, but I couldn't help wondering if part of him was relieved. I know he would never want any harm to come to me and in his way he cared for me, but he was never enthusiastic about the pregnancy so maybe it was fate intervening. In early February we met and went for a coffee to talk things through. But I realised then that my life and his life were worlds apart.

I was genuinely sad but I knew I had to end it there and then for good.

'We are finished,' I said with regret. That was the last time we spoke and I really felt that part of my life was over. Part of me will always love Ben and for a while I wished things had worked out differently for us but everything happens for a reason and for us things were not meant to be.

A few weeks later I was in a club with some friends. It was the hen night of one of my best friends, in Portugal. Everyone was enjoying themselves and there were couples everywhere. I couldn't help but think I should have been there with Ben. I missed the good times we had. When Adele's song 'Someone Like You' came on I couldn't stop the tears. I was swept away on a wave of regret. My friend took my hand, she knew exactly why I was crying.

'I know you loved him Gemma,' she said. 'Give it time, you'll be OK.'

I felt stupid but I cried for about half an hour. I let everything out. I was crying for me, for Ben, for our baby and for the broken dreams. I was letting go of everything.

Then I swigged my brandy, pulled myself together, took a deep breath and thought: it's over now Gemma, you have to move on. I still can't listen to that song without wanting to break down crying though. I will always be in love with Ben – well, a part of me will.

Looking back I realise that everything came along at the wrong time. Ben was very charismatic and I loved him but he wasn't the Ben I fell for when I was young. If *TOWIE* had never happened for me we would probably be together but I'm not blaming the show and I wouldn't have given up the opportunity for anyone. It was sad that Ben didn't want to be a part of my new life.

Spring came and I concentrated on resting. It had been a roller-coaster year and I needed some me time before I started back on *TOWIE*. When I did I was ready and raring to go.

Back on set things were developing between James Argent – Arg – and me. We had been flirting throughout the series and there was a genuine attraction there. I thought he was funny and charming. I had never been bothered about looks; for me it was all about personality and whether a man could make me laugh. Arg made me laugh a lot.

After Ben and the miscarriage I wasn't looking to get involved with anyone else but the attention from another man was flattering and I couldn't help getting caught up in it. The producers could see there was chemistry between us and as a result, we had a lot of scenes together.

In April, at the end of the series we filmed a Jubilee tea party and Arg and I shared a kiss. It was a nice kiss, there was no denying it, and I responded as enthusiastically as he did. When we kissed that night I knew it was the start of something. I'd always had a soft spot for him and suddenly we'd notched things up to another level.

I wanted Arg to work a little to get me and I was still not looking to get involved with anyone, so after filming ended I got in my car and drove off without saying anything to him. I wanted to leave the taste of my lips on his and an air of mystery. The party had been held in a stately home and Arg followed me in a cab down the long driveway. He pulled up alongside me and opened the car window.

'Gemma, where are you going?' he asked.

'I'm going home, Arg.'

'I'm going to Vegas in the morning,' he told me.

'What happens in Vegas stays in Vegas,' I winked. 'I'll see you when you get back.' And with that I drove off leaving him wondering.

The next time I was scheduled to meet him was when we all filmed the *TOWIE* Marbella special in Spain that summer.

In the meantime I got on with life and put Arg to the back of mind. In May I went to a singles night in Chigwell. I wasn't looking for love, I went with a friend. It was a new event being held at the Prince Regent. I met my friend Kelly in the King Will first. I was still slim after boot camp, and I was wearing a dress from Debra Chigwell, it was slim and fitted and I was feeling good about myself. I was going to be social, not to meet someone.

As I walked in the pub a good-looking man I had never seen in Essex before walked up and said hello. Initially I thought perhaps he was someone I had sold a car to in the past.

Then I realised he had seen me on TV. 'I really love watching you on *TOWIE*, can I buy you a drink?' he asked. I declined. He asked where I was going and I told him I was going to the Prince Regent.

'So am I,' he replied. 'Perhaps I'll see you in there.' He was dashing and I said maybe he would.

A little while later, when we got to the venue, he was there and made a beeline for me. He introduced himself as Rami and invited me over to his table for a drink. I accepted and we had a few drinks.

We got on well and at the end of the night we exchanged numbers.

The next day he called and asked me out to dinner. I was enjoying the attention and felt ready to get back in the dating game and start mingling so I agreed and over the following weeks Rami and I became an item. He was very kind to me and was smitten. I was taken with him but tried to keep things casual as I didn't want to get into any serious relationships. Nevertheless I would sometimes stay at Rami's house and he gave me a set of door keys. I really liked him, but I wasn't sure after so many heartaches that I could bring myself to get webbed up again with someone as I knew I was going away for a month.

I busied myself with preparations for Marbella. The summer was pretty much planned out. After Marbella I was due to fly to Ibiza to attend a boot camp there and then I was flying to Turkey for a holiday with Louise and her family. Trying to work out what to pack for a *TOWIE* Marbs special was a nightmare and in the end

I employed the services of two celebrity stylists, Jade Elliott and Fiona Parkhouse. They spent hours talking to me and studying pictures of me, looking at what suited me and what I liked and they arranged two suitcases of clothes for me which would be ready when I flew out. The service cost £1000 but it was a godsend.

A day before the flight, I was working in London when I got a call from Mum.

I could tell by the tone of her voice something was wrong straight away.

'Gemma, I am in terrible pain in Tesco,' she said. 'My guts are killing me.'

'Well forget the shopping,' I told her. 'Get home, go to bed and I'll come straight over.'

I rushed back to find Mum in agony in bed. Her face was pale and her eyes were sunk in her head. She looked awful. She was writhing around in distress.

I called the private doctor I had seen after boot camp and he came round. He couldn't be sure what was wrong with her and advised that I get her to hospital. I called an ambulance and she was rushed into King George's in Ilford. I couldn't bear to see her in such distress. Even today when I think about it, it makes me cry. I felt helpless, she was suffering so much I thought she was going to die. She was yelping with pain and nothing seemed to help it. After rushed tests the doctors confirmed she had pancreatitis, a very serious condition that can prove fatal. All thoughts of Marbs left my head. The only thing I was concerned about was being with Mum. There was no way I was going to leave her side. She had always been there for me all my life and given me unconditional love and it was my time to be there for her. It was terrible. I started to think what would happen if we lost her and those thoughts frightened me. I believe in the afterlife and I knew she would have been with me but I didn't want to have a life without her in it.

Mum was eventually dosed up with enough painkillers to allow her to sleep and while she was resting I called the producers.

'Mum's before Marbs,' I told them gravely. I really thought she was going to cark it.

The doctors worked to get her stable and she was booked in to have surgery to remove stones in her gall bladder. Three days after I was due to fly to Marbella Mum was wheeled into surgery while Dad and I waited anxiously in the hospital. It was the longest two hours of my life, and when the doctors came and told us the op had been a success and Mum was OK I sobbed with relief.

When she came round we sat with her and after twenty-four hours she was getting back to her old self. That's when I booked the flight to Spain. I called the producers and told them I was on the way.

Before I went there were a couple of things I needed to do. I booked in to the local beauticians and I had three layers of fake tan sprayed on because I was scared the other cast members would be browner than me and I'd look pale in comparison.

Then I turned my attention to my private life. I had a funny feeling that things were about to change and I was still unsure how I felt about Rami. I was going to be gone for most of the summer and I didn't think it was fair to leave him hanging on. I arranged to meet him in an Indian restaurant in Chigwell.

I explained the situation.

'I am going to Marbs, from there I am going to Ibiza and then to Turkey. I'm not going to be around for a month – my feelings for you might change but at the moment I don't think it's fair for you to wait.'

Rami said he wanted me and that I was his girl.

I gave him back his door key. I did feel torn and my stomach was in knots but as I left the restaurant all I could really think about was my mum and that I was feeling very anxious about her. I called my friend Alana.

'How do you fancy a trip to Marbella?' I offered. 'I'll sort out the flights and accommodation.' After everything I had been through with Mum I needed some support and Alana was like a sister to me. She was also a free spirit who enjoyed an adventure. She was up for it.

The next day we flew to Marbs. I had a quick meeting with the producers and an hour later I was filming. None of the girls on set knew I was coming. I walked in and they screamed. I was finally in Spain, everything was good, Mum was OK, Alana was with me and I was ready to hit Marbella!

CHAPTER TWENTY-TWO

DEEPER AND DEEPER

No expense had been spared to make sure our Marbella adventure was as blingtastic as possible. The Essex glamour had been transported to the Costa del Sol. I had a room in a ten-bedroomed villa that I was sharing with Sam, Billie, Jess and Alana. It was an amazing place, like something you would see the Osbournes living in.

I called home several times a day to check on Mum and she was improving by the day. I started to relax. I hadn't been on holiday for several years and even though we were called up intermittently for filming, there was still plenty of opportunity to enjoy the resort.

After a day or so I was called to film at the Sisu Hotel, a trendy boutique place with themed suites and lots of class. Some of the boys were staying there, including Arg, and we were filming at the pool. I was told to look as sexy as possible and wore a black Miraclesuit swimsuit with sparkles, a wide-brimmed hat and black sunglasses. A cerise sarong completed the look. I looked classy.

The producers, who made it their business to know what was going on in everyone's lives, sat me down and had a chat about Arg. They asked me how I felt about him.

I told them straight.

'He'd go out with me if I was thinner,' I told them. Although he never mentioned my weight to me, he told his mates and those conversations had been filmed and broadcast on the show. I watched them so I would see what he was saying. It never hurt me because I knew he fancied me but I thought he was taking liberties. It wasn't nice. And I thought more fool him because he was not helping his chances with me.

I explained all this to the producers.

'Tell him how you really feel,' they said.

So I did. I had my moment poolside. He was messing around in the pool and I strolled up to him, dropped my sarong so he got an eyeful of my curves and uttered the famous line: 'You ain't ever gonna get this candy.'

I didn't plan on saying it. It just came out. I loved every second of it. It was a very liberating moment and when the cameras stopped rolling Arg was like a kid having a tantrum.

'You've made a fool of me,' he moaned. 'How could you do that to me? You mugged me off!'

I laughed and secretly I knew he loved it. Arg would get so consumed by himself sometimes that he forgot he was on a television show.

I learnt later that Twitter had gone mad with comments after the scene. People loved the fact that I had stood up for myself and had shown off my curves with confidence. I had lost a bit of weight and I felt great about myself. I like to think I was speaking up for bigger ladies everywhere when I said that line.

The following day a dinner had been arranged for everyone so I texted Arg to make peace.

'Come on,' I wrote. 'Brandy, dinner. See you there. LOL.'

He replied.

'You've got a cheek. You better apologise to me. You're lucky I am even replying.'

We went to a restaurant called La Sala for dinner and Arg was late. I saved a seat next to me and ordered him a drink and two baskets of bread with garlic aioli. It was my apology and when he came in he accepted it happily and we had a good laugh about things. He was lovely company and it was an evening full of fun. At the end of the meal all the others were going clubbing but Arg put his hand on mine and looked at me.

'We're not going clubbing,' he said. 'Me and you are going out together on our own tonight.'

How could I refuse? He was wonderful company.

He took me to a bar and bought me a couple of drinks. I felt myself getting carried away with the occasion. The location, the company, the glamour: it all seemed too perfect. I started feeling strangely nervous. I was on my own with him and had always felt that I had the upper hand and the control over the situation. Up until that point Arg and I had carried out or relationship in front of the cameras or in front of other people, but at the moment I was on my own with him, just him and me. And I was falling for him.

'Have you seen the *Scarface* suite at my hotel?' he asked.

Arg knew I loved gangster movies. He did too, and he was staying in a gangster-themed room at the Sisu. I knew it was just a ruse to get me back to the hotel but I agreed to go back with him anyway. We walked to the port and got a cab to the hotel. Arg leaned towards me. He put his arm round me and pulled me towards him. I puckered up. We were like teenagers, snogging in the back seat.

When we got to his hotel we went straight up to his suite. Arg dimmed the lights and ordered up a bottle of brandy from room service. I wandered round taking in the decor. Everything was black and gold. There were black and gold satin sheets on the bed. On the wall there was a huge painted mural of Tony Montana, the lead character played by Al Pacino in *Scarface*. The brandy arrived and as I was pouring out two glasses the surround sound music system came to life with the Backstreet Boys song, 'I Want It That Way'. Arg was singing to me and he pulled me close. We started kissing and fell on to the bed. His hands started exploring my body. I responded to his touch. I ended up having sex with him as Al Pacino looked on from the wall. I didn't make a habit of jumping into bed with men but it felt right. There was nothing weird, seedy or dirty about it. It wasn't a one-night stand, I knew we both had feelings for each other and I'd known him for ages. It wasn't planned – I went with the moment and it felt good. Afterwards I was surprised with myself for going all the way with him but I had no regrets at all.

After sex we cuddled and Arg went out on the balcony to have a cigarette. I heard him talking and went out to see who he was talking to.

'You ain't gonna believe this, I've just had the best sex of my life with Gemma, but don't tell anyone.' He was giggling like a little boy.

He saw me and hung up.

'That was Mark Wright,' he said.

I looked at him and for a moment thought, I'm thirty, what am I doing? But I couldn't deny the chemistry.

'Do you want to go for a drink?' he asked. Jess was recording a music video in a nearby nightclub and most of the other cast members were there so we got another cab and headed off into the night.

When we got there Arg wandered off and started messing around with some of the lads. I looked around. It was 4 a.m., the place was heaving and I didn't fancy it any more. These kids are forgetting I'm thirty, I can't keep up, I thought to myself and in true Gemma style I turned and left without telling anyone. I sloped off and just left the lingering smell of Chanel No. 5.

The following day shooting was scheduled to finish and everyone was making their plans. I was due to fly out to Ibiza for a boot camp. Jess was going to Alicante with Carol, Natalia and Big Mark Wright. Arg and Ricky were going with them and they invited Alana and me. It wasn't a hard choice; exercise and rations in Ibiza or another week of partying in Alicante. I cancelled boot camp and told Alana there had been a change of plan. She was happy to come along.

Later that day Arg texted me and asked me out for dinner and drinks. As we were all leaving to go to Alicante from the Sisu the following day I managed to a book a room there for the last night and packed and moved in later that evening.

In the room, before my date with Arg, I had a shower and put on a silk and lace nightie, rollered up my hair, put on my face and body cream and went to stand out on the balcony overlooking the pool. As I was taking in the view I heard Arg's voice. He was talking to a friend below. I peered over the railing to see him and he spotted me.

'See you in your silk and lace,' he called up. 'Get up to my room now!'

He'd moved out of the *Scarface* suite and into the Las Vegas suite, which had a pole and a Jacuzzi in it. I felt a thrill of excitement. It was obvious what he was after. I snuck up to his room where he was waiting. I wasn't about to start swinging on the pole but Arg turned the Jacuzzi on and stripped off. He'd a few drinks. He got into the bubbling water and beckoned me in.

I dropped my nightie to the floor seductively and got in next to him. We had wild sex. It was mind-blowing and I could tell from Arg's reaction that he had never experienced stuff like it before. Afterwards, we collapsed on to the bed dripping wet and exhausted.

The following morning I got ready for the four-hour drive to Alicante and went down for breakfast. Arg followed wearing the hotel slippers. Big Mark organised us all. I got in a car with him, Carole and Natalia and Arg, Jess, Ricky and Alana got in the other car. Halfway into the journey we stopped for a picnic Carol had packed and the non-drivers had a few beers.

We reached Alicante by mid afternoon and booked into a hotel there. The clientele were mainly German holidaymakers so no one knew us. It was bliss.

Arg and I spent the next couple of nights going out together. We had things in common, we both loved theatre and performing and we shared the same sense of humour. We'd grown up near each other and knew the same places. I was thirty, he was twenty-four, but the age gap didn't seem a problem. It was a fantastic time.

One day we went out on a boat trip and Arg admitted that he felt our relationship was going somewhere. There were no cameras, no film crews. We were being allowed to discover each other naturally and it felt right. The only doubt I had arose later that day when Arg got a call from his ex and they had a row. I was a little concerned that he wasn't over her. I liked him a lot but at the end of the day I didn't want to be in a scenario where he was on the rebound and I would end up hurt.

Arg was full of compliments. He kept telling me how much he loved me with no make-up on.

The week flew by and I was sad when we were all leaving. We had all bonded during our time and the friendships I made on that trip I will always cherish. I had been swept off my feet by Arg. I'd never had a holiday romance and I could see why people become so engrossed in them. It was one of the happiest times of my life and we all knew it had been a special week.

The Wrights and Arg had an earlier flight back to Southend Airport than I did, and in the morning he knocked on my door to say goodbye. I was due to fly out from the UK to Turkey for two weeks in three days so I wasn't going to see him for a while and I knew I would be pining for him. We kissed and he got in his cab. He hadn't been gone ten minutes when he texted and told me he missed me.

I knew I had to wring out every moment I could with him and so I made a few hasty phone calls and rearranged my flight home to the one Arg was on. Alana and I rushed to pack and drove to the airport.

I ran into the departure lounge and flung myself at Arg. He hugged and kissed me and we flew back together.

At Southend we finally parted.

'I really love you to bits,' Arg told me and I blushed. Mum and Dad had come to pick me up and it was obvious to them that I had deep feelings for the new man in my life. I told Arg that I would see him when I returned from Turkey and I also made up my mind that I was going to find somewhere to live nearer him in Chigwell. Dad drove me down to Leigh-on-Sea and we had seafood on the prom. I was in a dream. I realised I'd had the best time of my life. I sat there eating my cockles thinking about Arg and getting a warm fuzzy feeling.

Over the following days I got ready for Turkey and also found a lovely apartment to rent in a posh development in Chigwell. The place was called Repton Park and it used to be a huge Victorian mental asylum. It had an on-site gym and spa and the apartments had high ceilings and period features. It was a rash decision, I only looked around quickly, but I put a deposit down and arranged to move in when I got back from holiday.

Arg and I texted all the time. He had gone to Barcelona for a few days with a friend. I was on cloud nine and set off to Kalkan resort on the Turkish Med with Louise and her family. I was looking forward to a calm two weeks and a chance to get back to some sort of normality. I had realised by then that my life would never be routine again. It wasn't the kind of life where I could wake up and decide if I was going to have a cheese or ham sandwich for lunch and that I was watching *EastEnders* at 7 p.m. Everything had changed. I was excited about filming the next series of *TOWIE* because I felt something was going to happen with me and Arg. I wasn't obsessed with him but I was having the time of my life with him and I will always be grateful that he gave me that when I needed it the most. After Ben and the miscarriage I could easily have slipped back into old patterns of comfort-eating and depression but instead I was full of optimism.

I'd been in Kalkan two days when Arg called.

'I miss you babe, I feel terrible,' he said. 'What would you say if I came to Turkey?'

'Yeah OK,' I said sarcastically. I believed it was empty talk.

'No seriously, I'm coming. Where is the nearest airport to your hotel, where are you staying?' I could tell by his voice he was serious.

I told him the details but still couldn't quite believe he would do it. He texted later to tell me he'd booked the flight and he would be there in a couple of days.

My first thought was OMG, I had no heels, no lashes, I'd had all my extensions taken out, I went there to kick back and relax.

A day later he called again at midnight but his tone had changed.

'What's going on Gem?' he asked. 'I went to the Indian in Chigwell last night and they told me you had been in there with Rami. I thought it was over between you two.'

They hadn't told him it was weeks before and he assumed I was in there during the few days I was in the UK. I heard a different side to the Arg I had fallen in love with during that call.

'Just be honest with me, was you having a meal with him?' he demanded.

I told him straight; my mum was in hospital and before I left for Marbs I went there to meet Rami and hand his keys back. Arg played coy and said he wasn't sure he could accept the explanation.

'I'm not coming,' he said.

I put the phone down. Part of me was upset, part was angry at him for not believing me and part just thought, I am in my thirties, I am older and wiser, I don't need the stress of it, if you aren't coming, you aren't coming.

I was left hanging and that night I went for a walk on my own around the resort. The mention of Rami had set me thinking. Had I been too hasty? Rami was older and more mature. He wanted to settle down. Maybe I had chosen the wrong man. I looked up and above me, on top of one of the restaurants there was a blue neon sign shining out against the black of the sky. It read 'RAMI'. It must have been the restaurant's name. I wondered if it was an omen.

The following day I didn't hear from Arg for ages but at 4 p.m. he rang.

'I've just landed,' he said. The cold edge in his voice I'd heard the previous night had disappeared and it was the old Arg on the line. My heart jumped. My eyes were bulging, my mouth was agape. I started running round the pool screaming. I couldn't believe he'd made the journey all the way to see me. I had to go and stand in an air-conditioned room to cool down.

Manically I started to get ready to meet him. I curled my hair in the 100-degree heat, put some mascara and nude lipstick on, found some travel lashes I'd luckily packed for emergencies and walked to the Elixir Hotel where we'd arranged to meet. It started raining.

Arg was there, soaked through in a white shirt and chinos with his bag. When he saw me he dropped it and ran to hug me. It was like a scene from a *Sex And The City* movie.

He was laughing.

'I just want to go walking with you in the rain,' he said, taking my face in his hands and kissing me. He left his bag at the hotel reception and we went for a walk, hand in hand. I was in a dream.

We were two lovers without a care in the world. We went down to Kalkan seafront and found a quiet restaurant. Arg asked the owner if he could put his iPod on in the bar. He chose a song and started singing Frank Sinatra to me. If I could I would have stayed in that moment for ever. Nothing else mattered, there was just him and me. I was in love with the romance of it all. I forgot about *TOWIE* and everything else.

We sat up until 5 a.m. and he kept singing to me. For the rest of the holiday we went on boat trips, we went shopping together, we did everything two lovers on holiday do. It was romantic and passionate and I loved his company. He paid for everything. I felt soft and feminine and womanly with him because I knew he was taking care of me.

One night we were in a bar and the football was on. Arg was watching and I looked at him and thought, I am so in love with you, this is the best time of my life, please don't ever end.

The game finished and we danced to Michael Jackson, 'You Are Not Alone'. I started crying.

'What's wrong?' Arg frowned. 'Why are you crying?'

'I am so happy,' I sniffed. 'I haven't felt happiness like this for a long time.'

He nodded. He was on the same page as me.

He had to go back before I did and when we said goodbye there were tears again. But I knew we were going to be together when I got back.

CHAPTER TWENTY-THREE

MOVING ON

Up until that point, life had taught me an important lesson: if it seems too good to be true it probably is. I'd forgotten that lesson and, in hindsight, I know now I had fallen head over heels in love with Arg like a naive teenager. I blame the glamorous locations and the holiday atmosphere. I think the sun went to my head.

For a time when I got back everything was lovely. I moved into the new apartment. The development was beautiful. There were BMWs, Mercedes, Audis and Range Rovers parked outside pristine new-builds with white picket fences. Despite the area however, I could never get comfortable. I had a bad feeling about the place. The energy there was all wrong. My psychic antennae were twitching. Because of what the place used to be, I was picking up on the negative energy left there by the former patients.

Arg came round the day I moved in. We went on dates. We started filming a new series. It was great for a while. We even did a joint photoshoot with a magazine and we had so much fun doing it, I really did feel that things were heading in the right direction and I think he did too, but then every weekend Arg used to go out with Mark Wright. I didn't have a problem with that at first but part of me wondered why he didn't want to spend the time with me. We had spent a month together non-stop and suddenly I wasn't seeing him. I was a bit older and when I had been in relationships before I was used to spending weekends with my partner. Arg was confused about spending Saturday nights together.

'Arg, Fridays are for friends, Saturdays are for lovers,' I tried to explain. But he had no concept of days and times – he could go clubbing on a Monday, Tuesday and Wednesday and think nothing of it.

Then the trust issues began to set in. Some photos of Arg in a car with a group of girls appeared on a website. He claimed nothing happened and that he'd just been on an innocent night out. I didn't know whether he was innocent or not and I wondered why he put himself in that situation in the first place. I wasn't comfortable with it and besides that, I was in love with him and I wanted to spend time with him, so why was he going out on the lash getting in cars with other girls? I started to wonder what had happened to the Arg who spent all his time with me in Turkey when we were inseparable.

We blew hot and cold. We rowed on the phone, we started filming, we were not really talking, the cracks were showing.

At one stage I hadn't seen him for several weeks and I called him. I didn't know where I stood.

'Am I seeing you, am I not seeing you?' I asked.

And then we patched things up. Arg was very good at romantic gestures. He knew I loved the Dorchester Hotel in London and he booked a weekend there with me. To say thank you I booked tickets for *Jersey Boys*, his favourite show. He treated me like a princess.

Then in August 2012 we filmed a scene in the bagel shop in Chigwell. It was a Saturday and the scene involved Arg, Tom Kilbey and me. As I was with Arg I assumed we would be together that night and I asked him what we were doing later. He told me he was going to a party at the Wrights' house.

'Brilliant,' I said. 'What time shall I get ready?'

He looked awkward.

'Er, you're not coming,' he said. 'I want to spend some time with Mark.'

'Spend as much time with him as you want because this isn't going anywhere,' I told him, trying to cover my wounded pride. I turned and stormed off, leaving him slack-jawed.

As I got back into my car, by chance I saw Rami; he was coming out of a nearby shop.

He came over. He was full of concern. He could see I was upset.

'What's happened to my girl?' he asked. 'When I see you on the telly all you do is cry.' He was right. There were so many ups and downs between me and Arg and the show always seemed to highlight the lows. I understood why – it added to the drama and made good viewing. But everyone was worrying about me and my frequent tears were being talked about all over Twitter and the press.

I felt at a low ebb: my relationship was turbulent, I had just moved and I felt that I was away from all my family. I felt isolated. I knew I wasn't feeling myself and I didn't know what was making me feel that way.

'What are you doing now?' Rami asked. 'I'm taking you for a drink.'

It was good to see a friendly face and I accepted his offer. However, we needed to drive past Arg and the TV crew so I told Rami he would have duck down in the back of the car. I didn't want anyone to know I was with him. It felt very cloak-and-dagger and as I drove past Arg I tooted and gave him the finger playfully.

He called within minutes.

'You have to understand I want to see my mates, what's happened to you? You weren't like this in Turkey?'

'Neither were you,' I retorted. 'It's Saturday night, I haven't seen you for weeks and you don't want to see me. What do you expect?' I hung up. Poor Rami must have wondered what he had got involved in. But we had a lovely evening and ended up in the bar at the Dorchester where I had been with Arg a few weeks before. Again I wondered if I should have stayed with Rami because he was older and looking to settle down. Nothing ever happened between us at that point; he was a shoulder to cry on. On the way home I played the *Jersey Boys* CD in the car and couldn't get Arg out of my mind. I felt torn. In hindsight I may have been expecting too much of him, but because it was such a whirlwind to begin with I found his behaviour now weird. I felt that he was pushing me away.

Arg made another gesture. He bought me a pair of kissing fish and delivered them wearing just a thong, serenading me. He knew how to get round me. He could be the most sensitive and caring man in the world when he put his mind to it.

We were playing our relationship out in the public eye and it sparked huge interest. That was all filmed and shown on *TOWIE* and it was then that I started to wonder whether perhaps Arg was seeing other people. Not a week went by without a newspaper or magazine article about us. I saw an article in a magazine that claimed when he was in Barcelona after our romance in Marbs he had been with a girl. He denied that anything happened but again I wondered whether I was wasting my time.

Away from the Arg situation everything was amazing. I was getting invited on to talk shows and panel shows. One of the highlights was meeting Louis Walsh at the ITV studios. I had been invited along with a couple of other *TOWIE* cast members for a channel open day and was in the green room having a lemonade when Louis bounded up to me.

'I saw you on TV in Ireland last week,' he said. I'd appeared on a show over there. 'You were great, I love watching you.' He sat with me for a while and we chatted. All the time I was pinching myself. I couldn't believe that Louis, an *X Factor* judge who knew Simon Cowell, Gary Barlow and Sharon Osbourne from the biggest show on TV, was talking to me. He went up to his dressing room to get ready for the show and a few minutes later his assistant came over to me.

'Louis wondered if you wanted to have a drink with him in his dressing room?' he said.

I was up there like a shot and had a great time. Tulisa came in too and said hello.

Back on *TOWIE* Arg and I were at the end of the line. He believed I had cheated on him, which I hadn't. Mario on the show had met up with Rami in a London casino and Mario claimed Rami told him he had been seeing me. Mario told Arg.

And on the show I was hearing too many comments about my weight from Arg. He commented that my thighs were bigger than his and in another conversation he said he would only move in with me if I slimmed to a size 12. It was all boyish banter and I knew he was only joking but it made me feel insecure. It was unpleasant reading criticism about my weight on websites and on Twitter without hearing it from someone I cared deeply about. It had all got very messy. It was a difficult time. I was very upset about it and was struggling to comprehend how we had gone from being so close to so far away in such a short space of time. It was not like in movies or the soaps where it is fake. It was strange and sad, I cried all the time. My reactions on *TOWIE* are the real me and the vulnerable me.

It was hard and emotional but in the end we had to call it a day. Basically it wasn't going to work out for us. I had a brilliant time but I had to let him go. I don't think Arg ever really understood the extent of my feelings towards him.

After the public break-up on *TOWIE* I went on a couple of dates with Rami. I needed to have some fun and Rami loves to party. I also enjoyed the attention. It wasn't serious at the time and I was cautious. For a while I still wondered whether I had been too hasty in leaving Arg. I had given him plenty of chances however. I had a moment of weakness a few weeks after we split when I was at a party. Arg wasn't there and called me up. He asked me go round his house. I'd had a few drinks and my defences were down so I went outside, hailed a taxi and went to meet him. I wanted to hear what he had to say. I needed closure.

He opened the front door of his house. He had shaved his head.

'What the fuck have you done?' I asked. He was wearing a free Channel 5 T-shirt and a pair of shorts. He looked like Uncle Fester from the Addams Family.

'There's some Indian takeaway left inside if you want some,' he said. It wasn't the romantic gesture I had expected of him.

I looked at him and wondered what I was doing there. I thought of Rami and how good-looking he was. He was good to me and cared for me. My rose-tinted glasses fell off.

'Actually, I've got to go,' I said. And as a final goodbye, 'I know you think I am mad but I really did think a lot of you.'

As I walked down the drive he called after me.

'I'm going to Scotland tomorrow, you can come if you want. But you can't tell anyone.'

I stopped and turned round.

'I think I'll take a rain check on that Arg. I want to be with a man who will be proud to tell everyone I am with him.' And with that I walked off, hailed a cab and went back to the party. I knew it was the end of us. Arg never saw me wipe the tears away. That time they were my own private tears, not for the cameras.

And, back home, with each tear I shed a realisation swelled inside me. I was Gemma Collins – an independent, intelligent woman and I didn't *need* a man and if I did choose to date a man it had to be someone who respects me for *me*. If they messed me around I had to drop them like a hot potato. All the heartache and pain I still carried deep inside me suddenly exploded into a burst of confidence. I'd grown up. I'd learned a lot and the one lesson I had to abide by was that I had to live my life the way I wanted to. There and then, I made a promise to myself: *from now on, the only way is Gemma.*

EPILOGUE

FOREVER ESSEX

So that's my story so far. Sometimes I look back and I can't believe that I'm the same person as the girl who dreamed about being on stage and put on dance shows for her parents on the dodgy living-room floorboards. Sometimes it seems so long ago, sometimes it seems like those years have passed in the blink of an eye.

The last year has been mad. If I think about all that has happened my head starts to swim. I'm usually too busy and I don't deal with things at the time. I don't get the chance to take stock and think about them and every so often I get moments where I remember things that I had forgotten: the termination, the miscarriage, the bingeing, the men; and it overwhelms me. I've had some very dark times and a year of depression. I think maybe I am prone to it. Even now sometimes I feel myself slipping into a dark place. I have times when I don't want to communicate with anybody, I don't want to see anyone and take to my bed. I withdraw. Basically, it just comes over me sometimes. Nothing will set it off; it is something that catches me unaware. I have never resorted to tablets. I pick myself up and get through it and try to stay positive and count my blessings.

The opportunities I've been given have been amazing.

My management team at Can Management have been amazing and I am now a proper businesswoman.

I might be a TV reality star but I have always had a strong work ethic. I have always had my dad's voice in the back of my mind saying, 'you have to work hard and earn your money Gemma.' So I am not the type of person to sit back and rest on my laurels. When my career on *TOWIE* took off I decided I still needed to work hard in case it all ends tomorrow. I wanted to put my platform to good use and make my mark on the world. I also wanted to do something for all the larger ladies in the country because they have given me so much support since I have been in the public eye.

My business idea came to me when I heard the inspirational story of a girl called Kimora Lee Simmons. She is an American model who put on weight, built up a clothing empire, met the man of her dreams and had two children. I have seen her on television and she is bubbly and outgoing. She reminds me of me. I started to think about how difficult it was for me to find clothing on the high street that reflected my personality.

Throughout the seven series of *TOWIE* I have been on, I have always had problems finding clothes that are glamorous and flattering yet plus size. I also thought it was short sighted given that the average size in the UK is 16 and getting bigger. So what did I do? In typical Gemma Collins fashion, I took the bull by the horns and sat down and started planning my own clothing range. I wanted to create clothes that were much more than oversized, boring, shapeless pieces of cloth. I wanted to change fashion for plus size girls forever. Soon, I'd worked up lots of beautiful designs and I launched The Gemma Collins Collection. Now, I have my own website, www.gemmacollinsofficial.com, which crashed within the first minute of launching due to demand. My gorgeous clothes are also stocked by Simply Be and available internationally.

I take a real hands-on approach. I spend hours sketching designs, choosing fabrics and photographing the dresses to make sure they are perfect. When I joined Can Management I teamed up with my manager Claire Powell and we now have a distribution centre and a whole bank of staff. I am so enormously proud of everything we have achieved. It's a dream come true.

I also have ranges of lashes, fake tan and perfume in the pipeline too. Times are very exciting. I love being on *TOWIE*. It will always be a huge part of my life and it's given me the opportunity to do other television shows. I am regularly on *This Morning* giving my fashion advice and helping other women to feel good about themselves – whatever their size or shape.

I still get offered money to go on diets but at the moment I am not interested. I would never say never, but I am who I am and I am happy and comfortable in my own skin. If people don't like that, it's tough. I'm never going to be a size 12. I still get nasty comments about my weight on Twitter nearly every day. Sometimes, especially after a *TOWIE* episode, I get an unbelievable amount. Sadly, it comes with the job. These bullies don't understand that I comfort eat in times of stress and they comment on me getting bigger which in turns leads me to get anxious and eat. It's a vicious circle. Some of the abuse is horrendous and even includes threats and swearing. I report and block them. But I know I'm not the only one on *TOWIE* who gets that kind of abuse. You have to learn not to take it personally.

There are a lot of women in my position however and I also get a lot of supportive emails. There is a lot of love out there for me and I feel privileged to be in a position where I can speak up for larger women.

One of the pleasures I've had is reading fan mail and messages from other larger ladies saying how seeing me on television has given them confidence. I'm really proud of that.

I know how lucky I am, in my work and personal life. After Arg I started seeing Rami again. He is a wonderful, genuine and kind man and even though we've had our ups and downs, maybe he will turn out to be my Mr Right. I will leave it to fate. I hope that I can remain someone who stands up for larger women and who shows that size isn't everything. I'm proud I have shown that you do not have to be stick-thin to make waves in show business or in the fashion world.

Life hasn't always gone the way I planned it and I've had my fair share of highs and lows along the way but, basically, I am still the same girl I have always been. I've had adventures, I've had drama; I've had tragedy; I've been depressed, I've binged and I've been bullied for being who I am but I wouldn't have had it any other way. Thanks to the support and encouragement I've had from my parents I know that whatever the future holds, I'll always work hard to make something of my life.

I still harbour that one big dream though. And, that's that I still want to make someone a loving wife. I still dream about sitting down to Sunday dinners with my hubby and two beautiful children. Until that happens my dream won't ever change. And wherever I go and whatever I do I will never change either. Basically, you can take the girl out of Essex, but you can't take Essex out of the girl.

ACKNOWLEDGEMENTS

Thank you to Julie Childs. Without you I wouldn't have had the amazing opportunities I have been given. I owe you everything. Thanks to my *TOWIE* family. I have made some firm friends for life in some of you. You've all touched my life. I'd like to thank Gyles, Mike, Mica, Ruth, Tony and Claire at Lime Pictures for giving me the most wonderful adventure of my life and anyone who has ever worked on *TOWIE*. Shirley, Laura and Jenna, thank you for everything you have done for me.

Thank you to Mark Thomas, you know I love you really. Thank you to *Closer* magazine and Katie Banks for all the laughs. Thank you to Claire Powell, Gemma Wheatley and all at CAN Management, my management team, for pushing me and thank you to the powers that be at *This Morning* who gave me the dream job of my life presenting on the show. Thanks to Ruth and Eamonn who are like my TV parents and to Peter Fincham at ITV for believing in me.

Thank you to Kelly Ellis and everyone at Ebury for making this book happen and special thanks to Nick Harding, it's been a joy and a pleasure working with you.

To all my friends, who have touched my life. I can't wait for the day when we are all pensioners sitting round the table drinking tea and laughing about the good times. Vicky, Alana, Louise, Cassie, Lisa and Jeff I couldn't have wished for better soulmates. Thank you for all of your sensible advice and strength. Rene and Claire, you have always helped me and been there for me.

I would like to say a special thank you to the best girl in the world Louise Morgan; you don't know how much you mean to me. You are the best friend a girl could wish for. I will always love you and Poppy.

Thank you to all of my family and special thanks to my dad. Thank you for your wisdom and spiritual teaching. I only hope that whoever I end up settling down with will have the same qualities as you. Wisdom, kindness and strength. Without you and Mum I wouldn't be where I am today.

Thank you so much to all my fans, my love for you is unconditional.

To everyone in my life, you're all invited to the party when I've cracked it and bought my villa in Spain!